Shoes to Live in Iowa...
by John Ellerbach
illustrated by
Scott Fabritz

Copyright © 1986 by John Ellerbach

All rights reserved. No part of this book may be used or reproduced in any manner without written permission of the publisher, John Ellerbach. Brief excerpts for reviews are excepted.

Layout and design by Mike Cassler
Cover illustration by Scott Fabritz
Proofreader: Kelley Jones
Dedicated to Andi

Ordering information: Send $4.95 (plus 20 cents tax in Iowa) for each book to John Ellerbach, 878 41st St., Des Moines, IA 50312

Parts of some of the essays were previously published in *Progress* and *Des Moines* magazine.

ISBN 0-9616813-0-6

Contents

Forewarned, by Donald Gull....................................page 0
Try the I-Place for Size..page 2
Is This How the Soaps See Us?..............................page 4
The Naked Car Wash..page 6
Homeclowning '88..page 9
Shoes to Live in Iowa..page 12
When and Where to Tour in the Buckeye State,
by P.R. Gladhand..page 15
Winter Cleaning..page 22
Of Doodles and Doggerel......................................page 24
Night Fishing in Iowa..page 27
Metro Iowa, by Sunny Cal....................................page 31
An Insider's Tour of Des Moines............................page 39
Driving in Des Moines..page 42
The Newspaper Iowa Descends Upon........................page 46
A Cartographer's Dream......................................page 52
No Longer a Forbidden World................................page 56
Real Men Mow and Fry Out..................................page 59
The Heavyweight State..page 62
The "Shoes" Comprehensive Exam............................page 65
Index..page 69

Forewarned

by Donald Gull

There's a tad of the gushy Iowa lovebird in each of us, as well as the crotchety old coot. But we're all good eggs and it's a rare bird that won't enjoy something in Shoes to Live in Iowa. Not since my hilarious book, How to Light on a Water Heater and Other Warm Stories, has anyone offered such insight on the Hawkeye State or feathered the nest with such fine frivolity for the flighty.

The author can be considered versatile or schizophrenic, depending on your perspective. Of course, if you know him personally, there is no question as to the answer. First off, he mixes metaphors unashamedly—shoes and birds. As you know, shoes and birds don't mix.

Add another peculiarity: He seems to be flying high on Iowa and suddenly he hires a New Yorker and a Californian to handle the tourism articles. Chicken!

Yes, to say Shoes to Live in Iowa is for the birds would be an understatement. Here's what's ahead:

All you loons out there will certainly want to read Homeclowning '88, as the many yuks that left Iowa are invited back to the land of corn. If you consider yourself something of a cuckoo, you won't want to miss The Heavyweight State, a spoof on how to turn those spare pounds into dollars and revive the Iowa economy.

Mockingbirds will immediately turn to The Newspaper Iowa Descends Upon. I read that one first. And snowbirds, shovelers and snowy regrets who detest winter will appreciate Winter Cleaning.

Secretary birds, do you have a booby for a boss? Read about a rite of an Iowa spring in Of Doodles and Doggerel.

Passenger pigeons, don't get into your cars until you've perused Driving in Des Moines. And terns can expect to go

Forewarned

around in circles unless they refer to *An Insider's Tour of Des Moines.*

P.R. Gladhand hardly parrots those sweet-sounding Chamber of Commerce brochures in his *When and Where to Tour in the Buckeye State.* Similarly, west coaster Sunny Cal offers surprising insights into our cities in *Metro Iowa.* Read it for a lark.

Real men, it would be a cardinal sin if you didn't read *Real Men Mow Lawns and Fry Out* and *A Cartographer's Dream.* Furthermore, find out what the author is grousing about in *No Longer a Forbidden World,* and dive right into *Night Fishing in Iowa.*

The bill of fare for shoebills, of course, is the essay upon which this book's title is based. And snipes and rooks will be easily recognized in *Life in the I-Place,* where the author says he'll warble about the good life here, but he reserves the right to screech about the pitfalls as well. It's a mellow song he whistles in *The Naked Car Wash,* and if you swallow his reasoning, he'll have you raven about Iowa.

Thrashers will particularly enjoy *Is This How the Soaps See Us?* And all you hearty bullflinches will smile and snicker at *The "Shoes" Comprehensive Exam.*

The silly, the sublime. The droll, the daring. "Shoes" is something to crow about.

Try the I-Place for Size

Are you old enough to remember the Pleistocene Age? How about the Iron Age? Or the Permanent Press Age? Today, we're in the Alphabet Age. Witness the A-Team, the H-Bomb, the N-Ban, the G-String, the C-Spot (with a children's version — the C-Spot-Run!) and now...the C-Zone!

According to a Californian who made up the term, the C-Zone is a place in the mind, a feeling of sorts, the epitome of peak performance under pressure. The C-Zone is doing your best with minimal stress. The "C" stands for confidence, commitment and control. It also stands for clownish common sense.

In the Alphabet Age, we love to pay premium dollar to be told the obvious. A magazine cover touts TEN WAYS TO SAVE YOUR LIFE ON THE ROAD; the article tells you to wear your seat belt, keep your car mechanically sound, and don't exceed the speed limit. A book for $14.95 sells MEGASEX: BEYOND SENSUALITY; the biggest idea in the book can be boiled down to "devote extra time to your lover and don't forget to nibble on an ear lobe occasionally." A TV newscaster does a series on RAGS TO RICHES: ULTRA-INVESTMENT OPTIONS; in his last segment he concludes that your best op-

H — BOMBS PARTICIPATING IN AN N-BAN

tion may be to put your bucks in the bank. Thanks for the help.

When I was thinking of a title for this book, I was tempted by MEGA-YUKS: BEYOND THE S-SPOT! ("S" stands for "silly") and FROM GAGS TO RICHES: READ 'EM AND REAP! But I'm not one for superlatives. Nor do I enjoy writing puffery. Therefore, I am not going to purport that the I-Place, Iowa, is the mega-best place in the world to live. And I won't say that it's the ultra-spot for tourists. I will even say that one touristy piece hawking the "soothing harmony, the at-peace-with-oneself attitude, and the hospitality of Iowa and her people" is overkill, although it does contain some truth. In an age possessed by the "best", and the "biggest", I am content to say that Iowa is "pretty darn good" and "just about the right size." O.K., I went a bit overboard in "Naked Car Wash," but when you're away from home, you tend to get sappy. Likewise, P.R. Gladhand's article on Iowa's attractions and Sunny Cal's piece on cities exaggerate. Gladhand lives in New York, but assured me he has an extensive file on Iowa. Cal resides on the west coast, but she once spent a week in Minnesota. I didn't have much time to check their work, but both are supposed to be the best and biggest names in tourism journalism. And they spend a lot of time in the C-Zone.

In the C-Zone, people appreciate a can-do attitude, prize a sense of risk taking and applaud visualization of goals. It occurs to me that many Iowans have been in the C-Zone for years.

C-Zoners do a lot of what they call "awfulizing," or working through "worst case" scenarios. Big innovation. My sister taught me to awfulize years ago. Example: *"What's the worst possible thing that could happen to you, Johnny, if you dawdle on the way to church? You could be knocked senseless by a semi, fall into a sewer, be washed away to the Mississippi, be devoured by sharks (yes, there are sharks in the Mississippi!) and eventually burn in the fires of hell."*

See? Things aren't so bad. Once you arrest optimism, everything gets easier. And to this day I am never late for church.

So what's the worst that could happen to Iowa? We've been knocked senseless by the economy, washed away by doubt and devoured by the loan sharks. But we're still laughing! That's what I like about the I-Place. It's a pretty good place to be during the Alphabet Age, and it's just about the right size.

Is This How the Soaps See Us...?

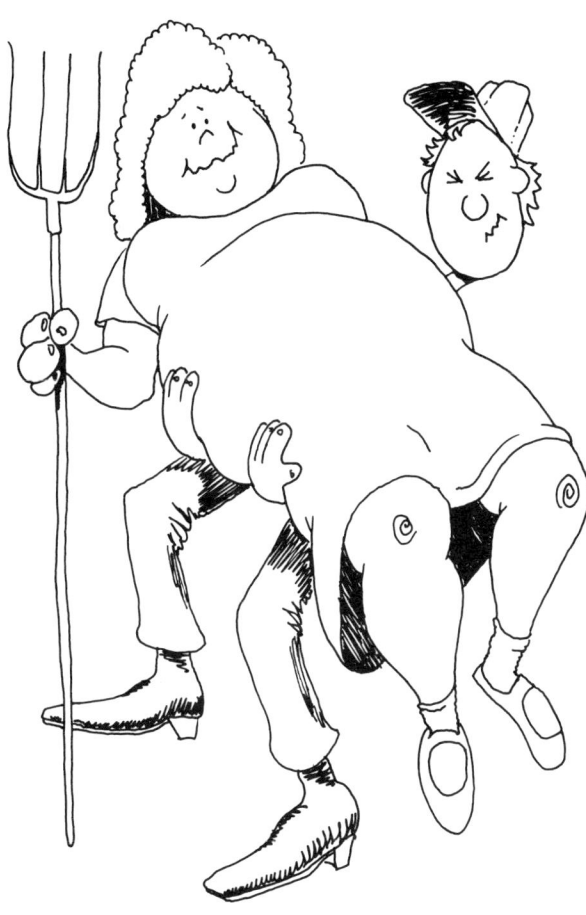

ONE WIFE TO LIFT

First we had "F.I.S.T." Then "Country." Then rumors that a monster might eat Muscatine. Iowa goes Hollywood. And we love it!

Even our kids get caught up in the fantasy: "Dad, you know what I wanna be when I grow up? I wanna be...an extra!" (That's what I like about Iowa kids: Their fantasies are tempered with realistic expectations.)

Why has Iowa drawn such sensational celluloid? Well, movie moguls and TV's top dogs recognize the need for realism and the resurgence of down-home values and clean living. And we love it!

There are, however, drawbacks to the fame and fortune that Hollywood affords our state. What do we sacrifice to the insatiable video appetite? Alas, our realistic expectations. We tend to be painted with the broad brush of stereotype. But it doesn't seem to bother us much. They write the script in faraway California, but when they get here, they'll make the necessary changes. Right?

Hollywood has asked me to comment on the following script proposal synopses. The "soaps" are intent on filming on location. "Have we captured the essence of Iowa?" they ask. "Are ours realistic expectations?"

The Young and the Worthless: A heart-rending tale of foreclosure and occasional rootworm. Oh, young Buck Sodfrill is doing very well on his farm, but he's torn between a love of the soil and squandering his money on an all-consuming vice — a lingerie boutique.

All My Chitlins: Young restaurateur settles in Iowa but thinks he's in the Deep South. Hilarity abounds as he attempts to master the native tongue and constantly puts the accent on the wrong syllable when pronouncing "Pottawattamie" or "Madrid."

As Merle Turns: Merle, a typical Iowa farmer, is filmed getting his usual 12 hours of shut-eye before spending a typical day on the tennis court and in the hot tub.

One Wife to Lift: Edna hit the potlucks pretty heavy over the winter and Earl accepts a bet that he can still hoist her over his head. Dramatic dialogue: "Hell, if I can chuck four hay bales, I can handle Edna!" Suspense.

Another Nerd: Posing as a hayseed Iowan is Dirk "Interstate 80" Archer, a handsome boy with a hankering for Shazam Sheherezade, farm wife and temptress. But she sees Dirk as just another pair of cute ears under a seed corn cap...

The Guiding Blight: Adversity abounds. George Boar becomes the self-appointed protector of the raging stinkweed. But the pollen count is up and the town is up in arms. Will George hold fast to his "live and let live" value system — or will he succumb to the temptation of a cheap defoliating agent?

Search for the Day Before Yesterday: Jake and Cy seem to be placidly playing checkers, but the ongoing feud erupts: "I seen Merle down at the Polo Club the day before yesterday!"

"Weren't not! You might'a seen him getting a manicure at Sodfrill's boutique a week ago..." The show is rife with royal conflict: "King me!"

Dullest: Several Iowa communities compete with a contained passion for the distinction of being named the most laid-back town in America. Oil is discovered and a Jedd Clampett look-alike contest yields some surprises. (Caution: For the timid).

Diner-Sty: Illegitimate offspring, a nervous collapse and a seductive hog named Krystle haunt Arnold, the lovable pig resurrected from the realistic "Green Acres" show. Arnold tries to forget by opening a truck stop. Nearly three million Iowans are recruited for guest appearances.

So that's how the soaps see Iowa. Are they on target? I'm going to give them an unqualified "Yes" — if they'll promise to use me as an extra...

The Naked Car Wash

"How many naked car washes does Iowa have?"

I'll never forget that inquiry — especially since it was offered with such matter-of-fact innocence.

I used to teach conversational English in Lima, Peru. I was continually flattered by my students' resolve to master "the most important language in the world" and to corner this native speaker at every opportunity to practice it. I also was amazed that a depth of knowledge and a superficial understanding of the United States could co-exist in those same inquisitive minds. On one hand, some students knew more about U.S. history than I did. On the other hand, they knew little about modern American culture. They got their impressions of contemporary U.S.A. from three primary sources: newspaper stories, dubbed reruns of "I

Love Lucy" and "Dallas", and the movies — especially a series of films called "Asi Es America", roughly, "Here's What America Is Like."

I faithfully attended each segment of "Asi Es America" and learned more about the oddities of my nation than I had in 30-odd years of living here.

My students were particularly interested in Iowa because: 1.) They claimed they had never met an Iowan before. 2.) Had they encountered an Iowan, he would have been very tempted to claim he was from New York City, Hollywood or Miami because — 3.) New York City, Hollywood, and Miami are prestigious places to be from in the eyes of Peruvians. (One person not in my class did ask if I knew J.R. Ewing. I was a *real* American, wasn't I? Of course, I said, "Yes," and smiled. Any other answer would have been a letdown.)

My first hurdle was to debunk the American stereotypes in "Asi Es America." Americans are depicted as ultra-handsome, filthy rich and highly hedonistic. My humble presence in Peru should have instantly shattered the stereotype. It did not. Believe me, it isn't easy to divest oneself of purported lusts and riches; it would have been much easier to wear the cloak of fantasy than to reveal the naked truth. It was the car wash question that convinced me to tell them about the real America and an Iowa where polygamists, high rollers and merchants of immense greed are atypical.

At this point you may be thinking, "What exactly is a naked car wash and why are your students making such a big deal of it? Do Peruvians clothe their cars?" According to "Asi Es America," every city in the U.S.A. employs naked men and women to frolic in the suds as cars are automatically scrubbed and buffed bumper to bumper. The patron sits back all bug-eyed, wipers at top speed, as he's tugged through visual ecstasy. (For a few extra bucks, I believe, you can get out and help.) To my knowledge, we don't have those yet in Iowa.

"How far are you from New York, Hollywood and Miami?" asked a student.

"Far enough," was my reply as I launched into an explanation of the differences in crime rates, the overcrowding in the big cities, the traffic jams. I explained the happiness of fresh air, the green splendor of the countryside and the ease of getting to work in less than ten minutes.

"But why Iowa?" shot a voice from the back of the room in perfect English. "No neon streets, no all-night gambling, no drive-up divorces?"

Iowa was hard for them to understand but not to appreciate. Lima is a city of cement and six million people. Any vegetation that grows there must be pampered daily by a dedicated gardener. Many of my students had spent most of their lives in that city — an over-crowded, impoverished city.

In many ways, my students were like some Iowans: friendly and unassuming, sophisticated without being pretentious.

It was a surprise when I announced I was leaving the teaching profession.

"What will you do?" they asked.

"You see, Iowa has an untapped market for naked car washes..."

PLEASE CONSULT COMPREHENSIVE EXAM QUESTIONS #5 AND #6 AT THE END OF THIS BOOK.

Homeclowning '88

The governor of Iowa is making a big effort to invite back all the jokes that in the past few decades left our state to seek fame, fortune, and the correct pronounciation of the word "wash," as in, "I'm gonna go do the *warsh*, Ma!" Here's who's likely to return:

The Pun Comes Home: Ousted as "the lowest form of humor" by governor Stephen Hempstead (who got his comeuppance when a holding tank for those afflicted with adolescence was named after him in Dubuque) the Pun has been in exile in Minnesota. True, you'd see a Pun occasionally in a newspaper headline, but the reporter who reintroduced it to Iowa would have to pay someone to check under the hood of his typewriter before he used it each morning. However, last year a general Pun amnesty was granted, which means they could all flock back from the Gopher State, where, according to a spokepunsman, they were never understood anyway.

The scene at the airport was touching, as Puns began to get a feel for Iowa. Whole families of Puns were United, unless they flew Ozark. In 1988, the worst of the notorious Pun family, the "Oh, Ick!" Pun, is expected to make a grand grunt and groan comeback.

The Simile State: According to information I got from a Pun, there's a movement afoot, or at least atoe, to designate Iowa "The Simile State." The Simile, long worshipped in California, said, "Like wow, man!" when he heard the news.

It was back in 1950 that the Simile was raising Puns on a funny farm near Marshalltown, hoping that his pet phrase, "As wow, homo sapiens!" would gain acceptance in Iowa. Instead, the Simile fell into disfavor with the State Bureau of Acceptable Speech and was charged with possession of controlled humor. So the saddened Simile fled Iowa like a booed comedian. He soon fell in with a Hollywood press agent who first changed his phrase and ultimately changed his life.

Soon in California every sentence was required to begin with the word "like." To say the least, royalties were appreciable. Even Iowans who write their own weddings owe a lot to the Simile: "Like do you take this significant other to be your life-mate, or like what?" goes the ceremony. The Iowa Bureau of Tourism, recognizing how we slighted the Simile, hopes to appease it with the new theme, "You're Going to Like Iowa—It's Like...IMPRESSIVE!"

IOWA homeclowning '88

One-liner Ready to Return: "I left a one-horse town that was so small," quipped the native Iowan, "that it shared a saddle with a nearby one-horse town!" The One-liner is eager to return; in fact, he's already got his deplaning speech written: "I'm really happy to be here. I mean that sincerely. But do me a favor. You know that Simile: Take my *like*, PLEASE!" Of course, the One-liner never goes anywhere without his companion, the Drum Roll. "I sure am beat!" is what the Drum Roll is expected to say after the long trip. And according to the One-liner, he had scheduled an uneventful plane ride, but "a funny thing happened to me on the way to Iowa..."

Exaggeration Adores Iowa. Really! Exaggeration grew up here but moved to Texas so he'd have more room to stretch the truth. "I'm so rich," he claimed recently, "I think I'll buy the Iowa Lottery instead of Trivial Pursuit. Is there really a difference?"

Exaggeration made a fortune in royalties from politicians and used car salesmen. But if you want to hear 'ol Exaggeration at his best, go to any tavern near an Iowa lake and listen for "the one that got away."

Irony, Understatement, Parody and others: The only Homeclowning holdout is that old fooler Irony who, ironically, refuses to show. Her half-wit son, Sarcasm, is expected to be here, however: "As if you bumpkins deserve me!" he said.

Understatement is holding back on an answer, waiting to be certain he's not booked on the same flight with overbearing Exaggeration, who invariably puts him in a bad humor. "Iowa, isn't that a state with agrarian ties?" Understatement asked recently.

The Tom Swiftie is looking forward to HOMECLOWNING '88, especially after his friend Understatement told him Iowa was "having less than a perfect farming year." "Give it to me on the level," the Tom Swiftie said flatly.

Parody doesn't travel alone; she'll return with Madame Malapropism, her spokesperson who said recently, "Dame Parody is impreviously cognicient of your IOWA BOAR column and, quite frantically, we think a suit for defecation of character is eminent, or maybe it will come pretty soon."

Timing: Finally, look for HOMECLOWNING '88 special events, including timing trials in conjunction with the Iowa Olympic Games. Timing is the essence of good humor, and the Pun, the Simile, and the One-liner are expected to participate. Exaggeration will not make it: "Do you know how busy I am...?"

There will also be a big stand-up bash at the Old Jokes Home near Keokuk. The famous Farmer's Daughter will be staying over, as will Rodney Dangerfield's wife (we said "please") and, of course, residing in the Old Jokes Home since its founding, the ageless Therewasthisguy. Oh, and lest I forget...this being Iowa, the corny joke will officially open HOMECLOWNING '88.

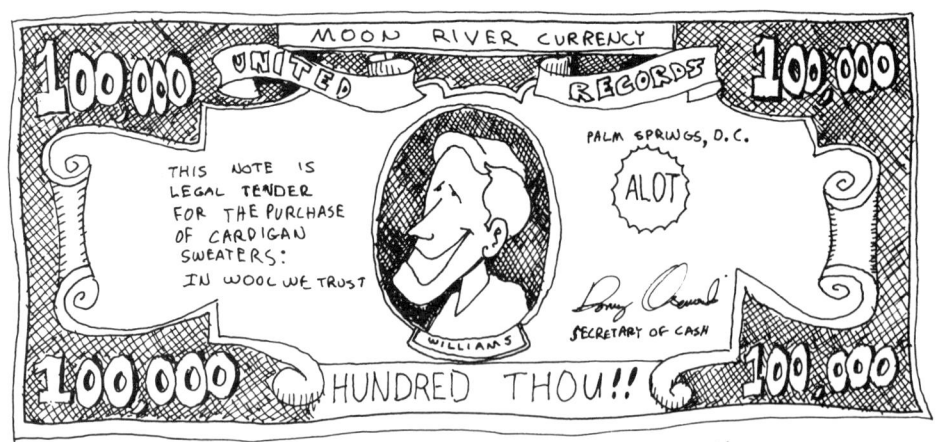

Shoes to Live in Iowa

Hats off to the high-stepping "Shoes to Live in Iowa" campaign; there's nothing shoddy about it. Fine footwear is putting some sole back into this state. Here's a sample:

Pumps Pay Tribute: "I'll admit it: I do get around and I like classy places. But I don't wear well on everyone and I'm not comfortable just anywhere either. Sure, I've put the pinch on my share of heels and I've put a few backs out of whack as well. But here's my posture on Iowa: This state gives me a lift."

Army Boots Give a Full Salute: "I'm not a mercenary; I haven't been paid to do this. But in defense of Iowa, I like her style. Me? I'm basic at best, but I've got a job to do and I'm respected here. Imagine *me*, me with not much luster and a lotta wear on the 'ol instep, right alongside those pumps on some shoe tree. That's Iowa for you: designer lines and a worker's pride — side by side."

Dress Shoe Shines for Iowa: "That kind of philosophy fits me to boot. This state's got class and this state's got pride. Sure, sometimes I'd like to step out with no strings attached. And yes, sometimes I wonder if one of 'ems going to burst under the pressure: They're a little worn but they're laced with courage...O.K., I occasionally date a polyester suit or I'm obligated to go out with a stuffed shirt, but I refuse to be dressed down for preferring Iowa."

Cleats Dig It: "I like to dig in and tell it like it is. You'd get a kick outta me. Granted, I was a little out of step in the Rose Bowl. Forgive me. But don't we have great fun on Saturday afternoons? I like this turf, too. I've got a foothold here."

Slipper's Soothing Remarks: "I've been chewed on by playful pups and trod upon by some pretty weary dogs, but I'm not complaining. Trudge the fields, pace the classroom, stand tall wherever you toil. I'm a warm fuzzy. So is Iowa."

No Runaround from Jogging Shoes: "I've been around the block a few times and I've seen a few things that really opened my eyelets. But you know what? Iowans are committed to health and fitness and I'm proud to lend my support. Here, designer sweats and cotton shorts run together. I look up to both of them."

Shoes to Live in Iowa

Toe Shoes Toe the Line for Iowa: "A few weeks ago, one of those snooty Eastern cutie booties blows into town, frowns and bounds all around. So I decided to strut my stuff too, and pretty soon it's clear I'm not a country clodhopper...But, in a way, I don't mind being underfoot — you know, underestimated. It makes the dance at center stage all that more rewarding. I've been known to leap from a polka to a pas de deux in a single bound. Not bad for a country girl!"

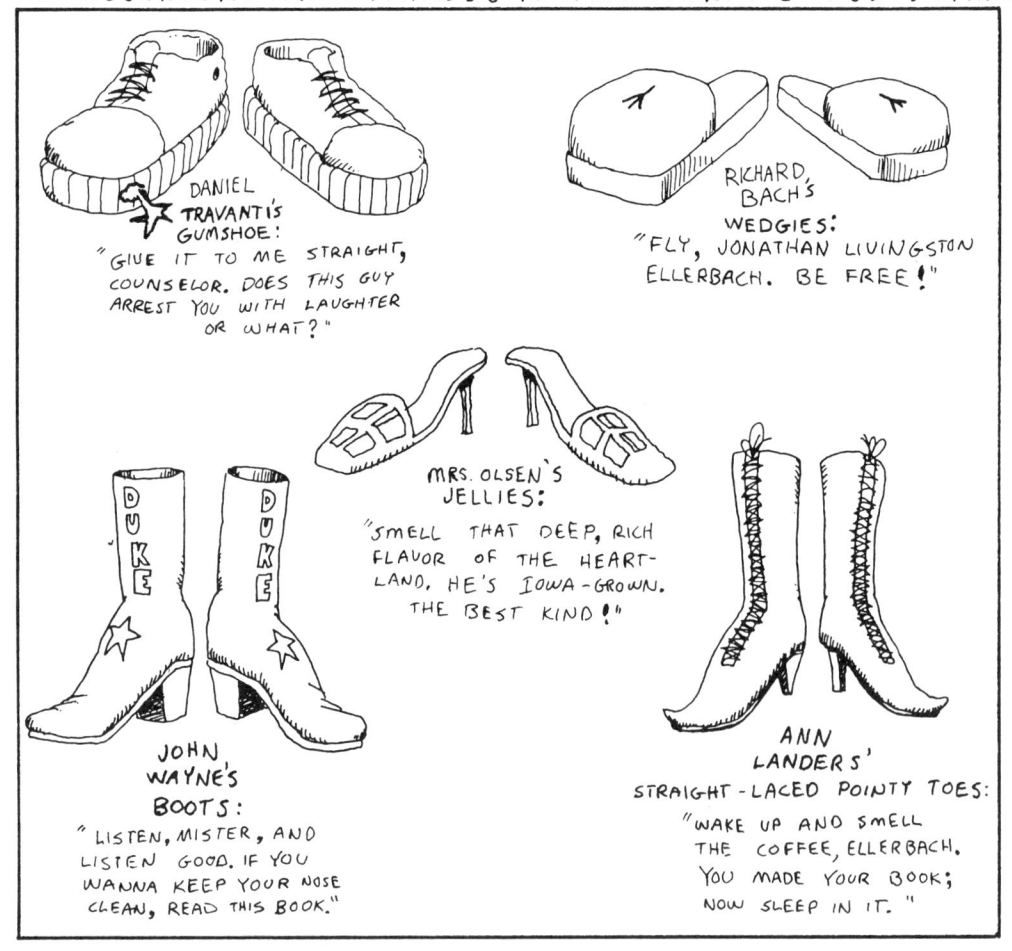

TRUE TESTIMONY FROM FAMOUS FORMER IOWANS' FOOTWEAR....

DANIEL TRAVANTI's GUMSHOE:
"GIVE IT TO ME STRAIGHT, COUNSELOR. DOES THIS GUY ARREST YOU WITH LAUGHTER OR WHAT?"

RICHARD BACH's WEDGIES:
"FLY, JONATHAN LIVINGSTON ELLERBACH. BE FREE!"

MRS. OLSEN'S JELLIES:
"SMELL THAT DEEP, RICH FLAVOR OF THE HEARTLAND. HE'S IOWA-GROWN. THE BEST KIND!"

JOHN WAYNE'S BOOTS:
"LISTEN, MISTER, AND LISTEN GOOD. IF YOU WANNA KEEP YOUR NOSE CLEAN, READ THIS BOOK."

ANN LANDERS' STRAIGHT-LACED POINTY TOES:
"WAKE UP AND SMELL THE COFFEE, ELLERBACH. YOU MADE YOUR BOOK; NOW SLEEP IN IT."

Field Boots Boast a Bit: "Yes, I've been known by other names; go ahead, you won't hurt my feelings. I've kicked a clog or two in my day. Like my army buddy, I don't do anything fancy in my field, but I'm surefooted and strong. And when the trail gets rough, I don't expect to walk off with any awards, but I've got some advice for loafers: Get some steel in your toes or take a hike!"

Loafers Lash Out: "I'm too casual for you, right? O.K., Iowa is a decent place...and maybe you're right: I need to hit the road. Maybe I'll return to appreciate the pace and my walk in life. I'm just tired of hearing that I should walk a mile in your shoes."

Galoshes Not All Wet: "Hey, don't get upset! I've covered up for some loafers before and, frankly, they're good for Iowa. They're not the only ones who can't stand the sight of me, up to my ears in slush, and "old salt" if you will, at times a drifter. They say if it weren't for five months of me, Iowa would be more liveable. Of course, they're wrong. I like to think of Iowa as well-seasoned."

Hip Boots Wade Through to Truth: "At first I thought, 'Who let the loafers in here?' But I've got to agree with the galoshes: No matter what our style, there's a place for us in Iowa. For example, I'm needed, especially when the politicians walk that fine line between truth and twaddle. I'd bet my best socks that Iowans never let the twaddle get too deep before somebody with down-home sense wades through it with me. That's the truth."

Extravaganza

The "Shoes to Live in Iowa" campaign may be just the beginning. In fact, the entire wardrobe may come out of the closet to be candid about our state. It could be a sartorial extravaganza. Imagine: Everybody and everything celebrating such observances as "Suit Yourself with Iowa!" "Iowa, You Wear It Well!" and "I'm Proud to Have Iowa Ties!" The whole darn outfit could proclaim "Make a Vestment in Iowa!" Tourists could be told, "Let's All Frock to Iowa!" Even the "unmentionables" might speak out; and your underwear could lend support.

Would it be long before not only ready-to-wear but other possessions as well began to put their best foot forward? What if our very abodes boasted to Iowa's liveability: "Our Foundations Are Firm in Iowa!" What if our cars revved themselves into a frenzy over the open spaces and lack of congestion? What if our tools and sporting goods and furniture all started speaking...? Wow. Then we might be needing some professional help...Let's not get too carried away.

When and Where to Tour in the Buckeye State

by P.R. Gladhand

I was flattered when John Ellerbach asked me to write this piece on a state so dear to my heart. Let's just jump right into the excitement!

January, February, March and April: Nothing going on. The state is completely shut down. The borders are insulated, the rivers have been drained and the cities have been boarded up. Everyone's in Florida, except for a few caretakers who bear an uncanny resemblance to Jack Nicholson in the final scenes of *The Shining*.

May: Pella Tulip Festival time. The tulip is the pride of Pella, and it's a real nice one. Sniff it and get silly. Some tulip-crazed natives even go so far as to put on wooden shoes and scrub the streets. By the way, there is also a tulip festival in Orange City, a northwestern Iowa town constructed entirely from citrus rinds. Actually, Orange City grows a single tea rose, but Iowans are so polite (and still not back from Florida) that they've never told Orange Citians the truth. Maybe one day a Bostonian will come to town and shatter the tulip dream that these people have based their lives on. Bostonians do these kinds of things.

One other note: Pella people and Orange City people hate each other. (You won't find such candor in other touristy articles!) Each charges that the other stole its tulip festival idea. The War of the Tulips has been going on for over 100 years now, with nightly skirmishes involving pistols and stamens and hump-backed and hideous Jack Nicholson look-alikes near Fort Dodge.

Also in May, **DubuqueFest** is billed as Iowa's largest Arts festival. Anyone named Art is invited to town (in Dubuque, all men are required to be named Art. Go get a phone book and see!) to be weighed. Prizes include free admission to a Dubuque City Council meeting and a tour of the famous torture chamber (no longer in use — whew!) at Wahlert High School.

In addition, check out the **Cherokee Memorial Weekend Rodeo**. Ever notice how easily a weekend gets away from you? Well, the innovative folks in Cherokee have found a way to corral the little sucker and hold onto it forever. Do you know what that could do for your golf game? Once you're settled in a Cherokee weekend, you won't want to leave. Of course, you won't be *able* to leave either. Then you start growing hair and a hump on your back...

June: Come help Cedar Rapids celebrate its rich cultural mix — they need the money. Each year an ethnic celebration puts the kabosh to notions that Iowa is lily white. Cedar Rapids boasts a Czech, a black, a Greek, a Dane, two Norwegians, and three Mexicans. And if you really want to ingratiate yourself with the natives, be sure to refer to Cedar Rapids as "Iowa's Second City" or "Not as nice as Des Moines, but you can't have everything!" Then hightail it to Jefferson to catch your breath and the **Iowa Pride Bell Tower Festival.**

This two-day June celebration centers on the worship of bells, a popular pastime of the Dingaling Sect, Iowans who can't afford Florida. You could ride to the top of the unique Myheyday Memorial Bell Tower, but it's only one story, so prepare to stand in the elevator a long time. This is a joke that the Dingalings like to play on people unlike themselves who get to go on a vacation. Tourists have responded in-kind, setting fire to the tower on several occasions.

Don't miss the **Grant Wood Festival** at Stone City this month. Marvel at the wonderful things the natives have made from a federal government grant of four billion linear feet of oak. The legend is that Stone Citians originally had applied for urban renewal funds but got the lumber instead. A good place to whittle away a weekend.

June also boasts **Burlington Steamboat Days**, where you can enjoy your favorite country western, jazz, rock music or traditional Inquisiton torture tunes. But the big celebration is a commemoration of the twentieth year after Burlington acquired its first steamboat, when a tired but enterprising Burlingtonian whipped the team of horses for the last time and said, "Hey, I've got an idea: Why don't we try this durn thing *on the river!*" For the next twenty years, they drowned a lot of horses, but that's progress I guess.

July: In early July, Clinton, a city north of Burlington, has its **Riverboat Days**. You can see Clintonians in native dress run down to the shore daily and shout, "Shucks, I forgot we even had a river! Is it wet or what?"

During **Creston Railroad Heritage Days**, the romance of the steam engine is recalled. It seems it had one of those memorable midnight trysts with a firey pufferbilly shaped like Joan Collins and just as ancient...

State Tour

EASY RIDER

Come to Waukee for the **Central Hawkeye Old Time Power & Machinery Show**. Given the state of Iowa farm economy, you'd better believe that the old implements are still in use. The highlight of this special event is that people drive their cars through town. Not since those Soviet parades through Red Square has there been such hoopla!

RAGBRAI: This event is named after the last-gasp utterances of a newspaper reporter: "Really...Ate...Good...Bicycle's...Rear...Axel...IIIIIIII! RAGBRAI began as a newspaper public relations stunt to convince the public that all reporters are not immoral, unathletic, cretins. "And this proves that we're athletic," said an immoral reporter.

On this bike ride across Iowa, people take plenty of cars and trucks. In fact, the majority of participants fasten exercycles to the beds of pick-up trucks and participate that way, sometimes even remembering to pedal as they wave at the farmers.

RAGBRAI, as the name infers, is Iowa's answer to the Bermuda Triangle. Nobody who has ever gone on this expedition has ever returned to tell about it. Some say there's a voracious ugly beast out there, similar to the Reagan administration, only without a smile. Others say RAGBRAI riders just keep on riding until they find jobs in Illinois.

And what would July be like without the **Sioux City River-Cade Festival**? Just fine, thank you. But this festival does celebrate the channelization of the Missouri River. What a miracle of modern technology! Now Sioux Citians don't have to leave their homes to see the river — it's on cable TV! Some watch it for hours on end, and when a fish jumps — that's entertainment, at least when compared to reruns of Dynasty. Not to mention all the money saved on mosquito repellent.

The River-Cade Festival is climaxed by the Saturday night coronation ball in which two people are elected king and queen of the Sovereign State of Sioux City, which for years has been trying to secede from Iowa but can't because nobody wants to do all the paperwork. Typical tourist literature says "the opening of barge traffic made this city the gateway to the waterways of the world." Who are they trying to kid? By the way, Sioux City's motto is: IT DOESN'T GET ANY BETTER THAN THIS?

Davenport's **Bix Beiderbecke Memorial Jazz Festival** is a four-minute observance dragged out to four days to take advantage of people hanging around the Quad Cities trying to pronounce this guy's last name. (His first name isn't that easy either. It's pronounced "Harold.")

Few people know that Iowa was the hub of the Jazz Age. Few people know this because it's a baldfaced lie. The fact is, Iowa would have missed the Jazz Age entirely had not Bix, in a pie-eyed stupor, jumped a horse-drawn barge headed across Iowa. (The barge was

A BIG WINNER AT THE IOWA STATE FAIR

reportedly full of the first round of documents for Sioux City's secession.) He blew one note on a French horn. One note. Not a bad day's work. Not when you consider all he got out of it: a memorial on the Mississipi and a museum. Check it out. By the way, do you think it was an ordeal in that one-story elevator in Jefferson? Was that Dubuque City Council meeting the worst form of torture you've ever known? O.K., it probably was. But a close second is trying to escape from Davenport without the correct pronunciation of Harold's name. They have check points staffed with linguists and speech therapists set up along all the exits.

August: Don't miss the **Britt National Hobo Convention**. Let me tell you, it ain't high fashion. In fact, it looks like downtown after the Sheboygan Rotary Club lets out. Five-hundred gallons of mulligan stew are served free to the public, most of which goes uneaten because people are too busy asking, "Where *did* you get that outfit, Dahling?" You can visit hobo jungle and learn about the hobo life career option or you can dodge fate and go straight to the **National Hot Air Buffoon Championships** at Indianola.

During the Buffoon Championships, politicians convene on a city south of

CATTLE CONGRESSMAN

Des Moines to practice the ancient art of evasive commentary before members of the press, who, by the way, can be identified immediately by their attire, largely procured from the flea market at the Hobo Convention. Anyway, politico finalists judged to be effusing the best bureaucratic, hyperbolic hot air are allowed to shake hands with each other at the State Fair.

The most remarkable display of craft and daring at the **Iowa State Fair** is the securing of a motel room in Des Moines. Ribbons are awarded annually to those few who accomplish this feat. And for a real challenge, try securing a room and simultaneously showing a hefty cucumber or a huge pumpkin that will be rotten by the end of the week. Ribbons are also awarded to those with courage enough to *leave* their rooms during the Fair. It's squatter's rights for accommodations, and anything goes. Tip: The best time to be at the Fair is on the middle Wednesday between 9:00 a.m. and 9:10 a.m. Before that, they're setting things up and you can't see much. After that, they're tearing things down and you'd only be in the way.

September: It's **National Cattle Congress** time in Waterloo. This exhibition is bigger than the National Sheep Shebang and better than the World Rodent Rodeo. We're talking impressive. We're talking a moo moo here and a moo moo there, here a moo, *there* a moo, *everywhere* a moo moo...

The **North Iowa Band Festival** boasts nearly 50 high school bands from northern Iowa and southern Minnesota. Mostly, the Iowa kids sit with the Minnesota horn players to keep reminding them, "No! Blow in the *other* end, the other end!" The Festival is held in Mason City, home of Meredith Willson, creator of the Music Man, Mick Jagger.

Ah, September in Oskaloosa and time for the **Pioneer Craps Festival**. Do you really believe the pioneers spent their time spinning, weaving, rug making, chair caning and rope braiding? Don't you remember: most of us are descendants of petty criminals, horse thieves, deadbeats, no-accounts and con artists who shot craps for a living. At least the people of Dowehafta County are upfront about the whole thing and once a year acknowledge reality by allowing about 4 million tourists to celebrate their heritage by shooting dice and each other.

At the end of the month, Centerville, Iowa holds an **Annual Pancake Day**. Have you ever tasted an annual pancake? Better bring that extra tube of Ora-Fix.

October: Don't miss **Ottumwa Oktoberfest**. A chicken barbecue and spelling bee (to see if anyone can correctly spell the name of the month) is held Tuesday night. That's nice, because Ottumwa chickens don't get out much and this is their chance to have some fun. All events, including the parade, are held under a festive tent. Head-high snow drifts provide protection from sub-zero wind chills.

At this time, Dyersville holds an indoor **Festival of the Arts**. They don't want to do it. If they don't, however, nearby Dubuque Arts-in-residence attack the town with scores of black felt paintings of Elvis Presley and dogs playing poker. Do they fight dirty!

November: Back to Dyersville: They've got the **National Farm Toy Show**, although it will have to be renamed the International Farm Toy Show since most American-made farm toys are now made in Mexico.

That brings us to **December.** They have a special event in Iowa called "Christmas" when everyone gets jolly and anticipative, as if relatives were about to end a visit. In Davenport, a truly old-fashioned Christmas comes to life one night each year as over 100 costumed volunteers recreate frontier and victorian Christmas scenes in 30 Village Shop windows from 6:30 to 9:00 p.m. Ah, the sights and sounds of an old-fashioned Christmas! In my mind, I see blue hues and hear the sound that brings tears to my eyes, "For ten minutes only, under the blue light..." You might be at the Village Shops; most Iowans will be at the K-Mart.

So that's an impressionistic tour, written from my plush New York penthouse. If Ellerbach would have paid me more, I might have tried to rough it and actually visited your Buckeye State myself. Then again...

Winter Cleaning

Caution: This essay should only be read with the warm, upbeat sound of the Hawaii-Five-O theme in the background!

It is said that Iowa has only two seasons: winter and road repair. This is piffle. Iowa has four full seasons: Winter, the Dead of Winter, Winter Cleaning and Preparation for Another Winter.

The term "spring cleaning" is often misinterpreted. It was coined when somebody noticed that before you can get all your sorting, salvaging and spiffing up accomplished, another winter "springs" itself upon you.

Winter cleaning season is when we unwrap the rose cones and air out the dog, in a futile effort to free flora and fauna from winter's terrible stranglehold. But beware. Sooner than you can say "Surf's Up!" (which, of course, we have no reason to say in Iowa anyway) the wind chill index is way down and you haven't so much as mulched a petunia.

What does Iowa encounter during the fleeting cleaning season? Mysterious winter relics and preposterous accumulations of an ignominious nature. Or, in other words, lots of weird stuff. A sampling:

ELLERBACH AND DUST BUNNY WATCH "HAWAII - FIVE - O."

Winter Cleaning

Under the snow: Most snow is gone in Iowa by July 4, appropriately named Independence Day. When the glaciation clears, a sorry sight of a shortened summer appears: Thousands of orphan baseball gloves lay saturated in back yards; the pockets have gone puffy and the thumbs are raw and swollen, frostbite on innocent cheeks. Nearby are icy mounds of bird seed, bigger than a pregnant chickenhawk. Hardy winter birds, including the state bird, the slick-back sleet buzzard, have a bad habit of kicking seed off the feeder as they wipe their feet. Such cleanliness costs them many a meal. And lest we forget...remember that garden hose abandoned in late August, when the first big blizzard hit? It's cracked and shriveled like a molting snake, but it invariably remains, hiding, the bare spot where grass it killed last winter used to grow.

In the car trunk: Forty-two pounds of pine needles. It doesn't matter if last year you had an artificial Christmas tree or if you've never had a real tree: Pine needles breed in dark car trunks. Also, here are two fifty-pound leaking sand bags for the traction you never got when you used the...there it is!....shovel handle to beat your rear radials when the radials broke off a tenuous relationship between the shovel handle and the scoop. And, of course, the hide-and-seek ice scraper emerges. No matter what you do, you won't see it again until the next winter cleaning.

Behind the Lawn Boy: The final pot roast. Because Iowa is a deep freeze for ten months of every year, you can store a side of beef in the garage.

Behind the furnace: The filter your three-year-old saw you install during Preparation for Winter. That finally solves "The Mystery of the Graying Walls."

Under the basement steps: At least one dead animal, usually larger than the side of beef in the garage. It probably found its way to warmth inside but fell victim to that cobweb you keep reminding yourself to clear out.

In the hall closet: Dust bunnies the size of buffaloes, cobwebs that could ensnare a wild boar and 137 individual gloves and mittens without a match among them.

In the bedroom closet: Fifty-five back issues of *National Geographic* you intended to read on long, winter nights. The top cover leers, "The Perpetually Frozen Tundra," which immediately explains why you and a lonesome dust bunny watched midnight reruns of Hawaii-Five-O instead...

Of Doodles and Doggerel

FIRST EVIDENCE OF SPRINGTIME IN IOWA

The stubble look is fashion;
It highlights locks and curls.
But is it right, I'm askin',
When we see it on the girls?
—written unashamedly by John Ellerbach during regular working hours.

Springtime in Iowa

This essay is about spring in Iowa, believe it or not. What do you do when you're forced to remain in a stuffy office and it suddenly hits a sunny 70 degrees outside? Doodles and doggerel, that's what.

Here's how to get away with it:

Get out last year's annual report. Prop it up on your desk and bury your face in it in case anybody walks by. Maybe they'll think you're studying the boss's annual message that nobody else bothers to read. Actually, you will be doing what the glamour magazines call a "make-over" on the boss's face. By the time you are finished, he should look like Miami Vice's Don Johnson, Yasser Arafat, or Ann Landers with five-o'clock shadow. If it is a complimentary make-over (Don Johnson) march right into his office and show him what you've been doing for the past few hours. More often than not, you will be praised for your creativity and industriousness and be given a raise on the spot. Bosses appreciate employees who offer suggestions on how they might keep pace with the times and improve their appearances.

What if the photo is not particularly flattering? (Arafat or Landers or a combination of both) First, be sure it is not flattering by showing it to everyone in the office and getting their opinions. Next, march into his office anyway. Chances are, he'll be too busy to see you. That's probably why you drew the ring through his nose and the arrow through his head in the first place. If, by some stroke of fate or a tattle-tale secretary, he will see you, do not panic. He will fully understand when you proclaim, "I doctored this photo just to illustrate just how perfect you already are."

Unemployment Will Give You A Lot More Time

Who wants to work in spring anyway? Unemployment will give you a lot more time for doodles and doggerel. But if you got the raise instead of fired, don't despair. After all, you're entitled to sluff off for a few weeks until Iowa spring fever is under control. In fact, it's a state law.

Now get out a legal pad and bury your head in that. If anyone interrupts, mumble something about a report deadline and keep writing. After all, it takes hours and sometimes *days* to learn to write springtime poetry like the masters. Remember, you were probably taking "Labor Relations" or "Finance for Light Industry" when I was taking "Elizabethan Sonnets" and "Eroticism in Early American Verse," although I believe there were a few inquisitive business majors enrolled in the latter. Seven hundred, if I remember correctly. So shove aside the statements and stuffy memoranda and vent your feelings about spring. A few tips:

1. Choose a contemporary topic with which you are most familiar: Of course, this would be the stubble look. You risked your job and reputation for it, didn't you? True artists are always risking their jobs and reputations.

2. Do not attempt free verse: They call it "free" because nobody in his right mind would pay for poetry that doesn't rhyme. Example: Words and phrases like "spring" "thing" and "spark plug ring" are romantic words that rhyme. "Profit margin" "mortgage" and "crustacean" do not rhyme.

3. Do not be discouraged by your first attempts: I'll bet you trashed three or four annual reports before you got the boss's picture just right. Hey, even the great writers' first drafts are hardly ever up to snuff. Shakespeare's "Shall I compare thee to a summer's day?" started out: "Zelda I think you'd look too chubby in a bikini." So keep at it.

4. Let your mind go. Some people censor themselves too much and never get those creative juices flowing. For example, is it wrong or idiotic to ponder why men don't grow whiskers on their foreheads? (Yes, of course it is. Try again.)

5. Think in "word pictures." Was it Will Rogers who said, "I never metaphor I didn't like!" (A little play on words for you English majors.)

6. Heed the Successes of the greats:. In other words, if it works, steal it. Here, you can steal the following from me:

The stubble look is here, by troth,
Just as barbers feared.
On some men what is two days' growth,
For me is a six-month beard!

Finally, there is the question of what to do with four months' worth of stubble poetry and illustrations. How about publishing a book, "Thoughts on Springtime in Iowa or Why I Regret Never Taking an Erotic Poetry Class." Or why not plaster your works all over your office and declare yourself creatively liberated this spring? Better yet, why not convince your boss that your doodles and doggerel belong in the annual report? Wouldn't that stark financial statement be easier to get through with a bit of iambic pentameter in place of the bottom line? And then there's always his "make-over" photo...

Night Fishing in Iowa

What represents the potential of millions of dollars to the Iowa economy? What more than any other undertaking reflects the hardy soul of the typical Iowan? And what draws the fascination and admiration of local and visiting masses? Hey, if I knew that, I'd be governor. All I know is what it's *not*. It's not night fishing. No way.

Iowa Invented Night Fishing: Minnesota proudly claims ice fishing; Wisconsin claims snag fishing; and Californians are constantly fishing for compliments. But how and why did the night fishing phenomenon start here — and is there anything we can do about it?

We're Industrious: We're so industrious that we felt guilty trying to fit fishing into a full day so we bumped it into the wee hours. (By the way, industrious Iowan Horace T. Setcherhookstupid, is honored as "Father of the Luminescent Bobber," which, in the eyes of night fishermen, is as awesome an honor as getting your antlers at a Moose convention.)

Night Fishing Catches On: Isn't it funny how a whole society can do something like so many mesmerized sheep and nobody stops to question it? This happened with night fishing. Somebody went out one night with his pole and one of those fandangled luminescent bobbers and came back and nobody called him a fool and the next night two guys went out and you can see what happened...

Has Anyone Ever Caught Anything at Night? No. Nothing. Not ever. Fish need shuteye just like we do. Yet night fishing continues to be the rage, perhaps the one activity that truly holds this state together. Iowa night fishermen are a dedicated lot. On a given summer's eve, you can see us three and four deep along lakes and riverbanks. Surface waters are literally ablaze with shimmering bobbers jockying for position. Lanterns and bonfires easily outdo the illumination of the Las Vegas strip. And the effect on the economy is not to be made light of. Cooler sales and dashes to those all-night emergency centers account for most of the bucks. This can be explained by a bit of wisdom passed on by my father, night fisherman extraordinaire: "Son, there is nothing better on a hot night than a tall, cool one — and nothing worse than a fish hook lodged in the thumb."

Here's the Catch: An Iowan did claim to have caught something a few years ago while night fishing. It seems that the fisherman had unwittingly allowed his beverage cooler to drift into the lake, an oversight not uncommon when merry-making night fishermen are more interested in watching reruns on battery-operated TV's than in riding herd over the essentials of midnight angling. Anyway, dawn broke and there was the usual assortment of orphan coolers thrashing on the waters. A spawn-crazed carp was reportedly trying to impress his girl by doing a magnificent surface jump when THUMP! — he was knocked cold by a cooler bottom. Snagged on a line, the fish was reeled in. Of course, conservation officials quickly disallowed the catch, but night fishing devotees outside Iowa (all 3 of them) are still abuzz about it and Setcherhookstupid's nephew is marketing a luminescent night fishing cooler with a bottom that's supposed to attract sex-starved bullheads.

MORNING'S EVIDENCE OF NIGHT FISHING IN IOWA

The Confidence of an Iowan: Night fishing in Iowa is like the lottery: The slimmer the chance, the bigger the thrill. Chances are that your everyday night fisherman is also a lottery fanatic. And speaking of slim chances, some Iowans go night fishing without any fishing gear at all. That's what I call real confidence. We Iowans are famous for that.

Removing a Stigma: Unfortunately, some outsiders believe that fishing is a lazy man's sport. They say that to avoid the stigma attached to fishing (which can also — though painfully — be removed at any emergency center) we do it under cover of darkness to avoid the shame. This is foolish talk. We do it then because it's a scientific fact that humans tend to lie better at night.

How to Night Fish: First, choose the toughest, most mosquito-infested underbrush you can find. If it is near a body of water, all the better. Remember, if you don't come out with enough scratches and welts, you won't have any proof that you went night fishing. Next, throw away those luminescent bobbers. Bobbers are for sissies. Real men fish off the bottom. And never ask your father, "Why do beer coolers float?" when yours is out in the middle of the lake and you are responsible for it being there.

Night Fishing Builds Character: The good thing about night fishing is that there is no temptation to be jealous of the guy next to you who is pulling in all the big ones because there are no big ones to pull in. Secondly, you can't be jealous because you can't even see the guy next to you. The lanterns, bonfires and glow from Johnny Carson are just too bright. It's like driving at night with a dozen dome lights on; the glare is phenomenal. And light intensity is a matter of fierce pride among seasoned night fishermen. Think back to when you last saw a photograph of somebody night fishing. You can't remember, can you? That's because there aren't any. It's so bright they haven't yet made a film speed slow enough to record the event.

How to Tell if You've Had a Successful Night: Four or five-hundred coolers backed up at a beaver dam downstream is as good an indicator as any. But remember: Night fishing fun is elusive. It's like going to the opera: Sometimes you have to ask somebody to find out if you had any fun.

Why Me? Why am I penning this erudite treatise? Well, Carl Sagan has his universe and Dr. Ruth Westheimer has her dirty talk masquerading as clean talk and I'd like to be regarded as an expert on something. Sex and the universe were already taken.

Another Youthful Anecdote: Instead of bragging about my first experience with the universe, let me tell you about the most fun I ever had night fishing, when my uncle and I and a hundred others helped capsize a boat.

Face it: Night fishermen hate boat fishermen, if, for nothing else, because they can afford a boat. And did you ever notice how boat fishermen have the whole lake to themselves but inevitably end up about two feet from shore, tangling shore fishermen's lines in their outboards and saying nasty things like Ruth Westheimer does but forgetting that water carries sound better than the most sophisticated fiber strands created by man? The tangles and the nasty epithets happened to us. And that's why we deep-sixed some boat people.

Someday I'll be in a Commercial: *Announcer:* "Iowa means corn and soybeans and hogs and literacy to most people. But out here it means one thing to these guys — NIGHT FISHING!"

On cue, Ellerbach pushes special Setcherhookstupid cooler into stream and hopes for horny jumping fish to hit. Wife puts another Dura-flame the size of a Volkswagen into bonfire and changes channel. Daughter gets into shouting match with four-hundred thousand other night fishermen who have lines hopelessly entangled with hers. All are using Ruth Westheimer-type language. Ellerbach hoists mug to illuminated Iowa sky, stares into camera and utters plaintively, "Ya know, are you *sure* it doesn't get any better than this?"

Metro Iowa
by Sunny Cal

I have to laugh at people who think all Iowa is good for is potatoes and at people who believe that Iowans insert "youse guys" in every sentence they utter. Youse guys should know that Iowa is a whole lot more than that. It has cities, for example, as the following shows. (O.K., I didn't have time to visit and verify everything first-hand, but I did make a couple of phone calls from my beach house and I interviewed some people on the Strip who said they knew Iowa intimately.)

Dubuque

Dubuque is now the only city in the United States without a direct connection to the interstate highway system. In fact, Dubuque has no highways at all. There is a bridge, but as soon as it hits soil, it runs into a tree.

Dubuque's area is barely an acre, but its 60,000 citizens make good use of hilly space. The city boasts the only habitable 90 degree incline in the world — where the inhabitants wear gravity boots and use more stickum than the entire NFL.

Like other Iowa cities, Dubuque has a Throwdabumzout! form of government. Dubuquers feel that on the average it takes 10 to 15 minutes for a new politician to become corrupt. They now only vent their frustrations at the polls, because their rollicking noontime radio show, "Turn the Sound Off!" was cancelled.

The Dubuque school system, by the way, is the finest in Dubuque. Dubuque also has three liberal arts colleges, also among the finest in Dubuque.

No trip to Dubuque would be complete without visits to Cable Car Square, Julien Dubuque's grave, the Old Shot Tower and John Ellerbach's birthplace, now a first-rate sanitary landfill.

At the foot of a quaint railway on a steep hill, the cable car route, you will find many homes converted into shops that sell nifty stuff found only in Dubuque basements. Further south is a limestone turret overlooking the Mississippi, the grave of the city's founder, Julien Dubuque. It used to be a popular spot for romance until Dubuque passed an ordinance against romance a few years ago. Fortunately, there is a place where Dubuquers can let off a little steam just across the river, called East Dubuque. Any remaining steam can be let off at select Dubuque lodging facilities.

Another big attraction is the Old Shot Tower, where the term "big shot" originated during the Depression, an era that Dubuque has managed to preserve to this day. Prominent Dubuquers used to ascend the tower to drink, casting their empty glasses down the shaft. The size of your glass was based on your standing in the community. Of course, the bigger the glass, the louder the "clank" for all Dubuquers and East Dubuquers to hear. Thus the phrase, "The bigger they are, the harder they fall." While some families had their glasses specially made and required three or four strong men to carry them up the tower, the Ellerbach family never owned a glass but once got to help carry up a 16-ounce Dixie cup. Hence, the name Ellerbach in German means "damn fortunate just to carry

NO ROADS LEAD TO DUBUQUE

someone else's Dixie cup."

It is a misconception that you must be Catholic to live in Dubuque. You can also be crazy. So if you are not Catholic, people will often remark, "Boy, you must be crazy to live in Dubuque!"

One final note: Dubuque has a thing about converting old mansions. Yes, they are required to be Catholic, too, and they're a bear to try to fit into a confessional.

Mason City

Mason City was settled in 1854 as Shibboleth, which means "place where we mix up some swell goop that hardens and holds houses together." After the word "cement" was invented in 1955, townspeople decided to change the city's name. But soon the name Cement was confusing. Somebody would say, "I'm going into Cement," which immediately conjured up thoughts of the Mafia and a river. Last year they changed the name to Mason City, which in French means "has no points of interest."

Fort Dodge

Built to protect the Sioux Indians from the settlers, the world's only two-sided fort stands here. Unfortunately, within a decade after construction, the settlers stopped trying to scale the walls and started looking for an easier way in.

Muscatine

Two things are hard to pick in life — a good spouse and a good melon. Muscatine is the good melon capital of the world. One out of two ain't bad.

Ottumwa

Home of Radar O'Reilly of M*A*S*H fame. Radar doesn't live here anymore, but his Teddy Bear is mayor and one of his hampsters runs a bowling alley.

Marshalltown

Unique among Iowa cities in that it is famous for being fifty miles northeast of Des Moines.

Spencer

The only city in the U.S. where every man, woman and child is unemployed. Hence, the television show, "Spencer for Hire."

Sioux City

"If you've never been to the stockyards, then you've never been to Sioux City," says the mayor of this fascinating town. Unfortunately, Sioux City has been hard hit by the end of the Red Meat Era and any remaining cows and pigs there can literally be carted away. Hence, the "Take Stock in Sioux City" campaign.

The Stockyards Station is indeed worth a stop, just to see what used to be the Swift Packing Plant. They called it "swift" because one whiff would send you packing in a hurry.

Finally, be sure to see the Floyd Monument, named after that amiable barber on the old Andy Griffith Show.

Iowa City

Iowa City is a university town. From the air it looks all black and gold. If you are not associated with the university in some way, you are not allowed to live there or even visit. The University of Iowa is known as a party school. Most of the rigorous course work consists of learning how to fill nut cups and punch glasses without dripping.

If nothing else, Iowa Citians are honest; they don't heap hype on themselves. Des Moines calls itself the "Surprising Place" and Cedar Rapids is the "City of Five Seasonings," but "Iowa City, An Excuse to Smoke Marijuana" has a forthright ring to it.

Iowa City is the home of University Hospitals, site of the world's first drive-up heart transplant. Also here is Hawkeye Arena and Hawkeye Stadium, where Iowans vicariously participate in the sweat, grunt and groan antics of hyper-hormoned, post-pubescent semi-literates (otherwise known as coaches).

About ten miles from Iowa City is the Herbert Hoover National Historic Site. Hoover, solely responsible for the Great Depression, is not pictured on any U.S. currency but did pose for a picture on an oatmeal box, which, of course, was more valuable than currency in his day.

This area is also overrun with the word "Amana," which, roughly translated means "I told you we could get away with marking up this trinket 500 percent!"

For the only meaningful educational experience in this area, go to Plum Grove, home of Iowa's first governor, Bix Beiderbecke. Known as Iowa's "One-Note Governor," Beiderbecke headed what you might say was a laissez faire administration. In his fifth term he was quoted as saying, "I'm governor of Iowa? Where is it?"

Cedar Rapids

Cedar Rapids was first settled as Rapids City in 1841. This was before South Dakota was invented. When it was, everybody picked up and moved there, except the oatmeal processors, who knew they had to be alone and downwind from the world. Also staying behind was the city's Czech population, but only the good ones. To this day, Cedar Rapids will not take any bad Czechs.

Cedar Rapids is known as the "City of Five Seasonings." Founded by the pungent Marjoram family in 1841, Cedar Rapids soon discovered that variety is the spice of life and allowed the Parsley, Rosemary and Thyme families to move in. There used to be a strong group of Bay Leaves, but they were taken out of the city before it was done.

In 1846 the City of the Five Seasonings was turned down as the new site for the state capital. It seems they didn't have any Sages, who to this day only live in Des Moines.

Five miles east of Cedar Rapids is the Indian Creek Nature Center. Promotional literature (which, of course, you should *never* believe. Believe me, I used to write the crap.) says, "Experiences range from sensory awareness of nature to detailed biological studies." Kids, this is a tipoff that there's nothing fun to do there.

Waterloo

While in Waterloo, visit the farmers' market. These days you can pick up a souvenir farmer at a fraction of the former cost.

What else can you get at the farmers' market? Hey, kids! You want some attention next fall in school? Other kids go back to Chicago with a few rock displays, some Indian arrowheads or maybe a gram of cocaine. Old news. You go back with a used manure spreader! You'll finally get the notice you deserve.

Adjacent to Waterloo is Cedar Falls, home of the University of Northern Iowa Panters. Panters are constantly out of breath from telling everyone that their school is just as good as Iowa State or the University of Iowa. This can be exasperating and disheartening, especially when most of the faculty and administration refuse to unpack their suitcases.

Ames

A third state university is located just down the road from Des Moines in Ames. Just-Down-the-Road-from-Des Moines University, formerly Iowa State University, is called "Moo-U," which some people say distorts the image of the university. Agreed. Ames students are a friendly bunch and therefore the university should be named "Moo-Us" or "Moos-R-Us."

Iowa Great Lakes

Not really a city, but as close as Iowa gets to a resort atmosphere, the Iowa Great Lakes were named by a New York tourist who said, "Iowa has *lakes*? Great!"

The big attraction here is Lake Okoboji, home of the University of Okoboji, my kind of institution. It doesn't exist, which means that tuition can be very reasonable. And it doesn't look bad to have a Ph.D. from the

University of Okoboji on your resume. Just tell your employer it's in Canada. They never check.

In this region you will also find Cayler Prairie, a native prairie that has never been touched by farming or development. Ambitious tourists who can't seem to leave that entreprenurial spirit at home will enjoy haggling for condo rights or permission to put a Pork Boy franchise smack dab in the middle of Cayler Prairie. The locals love the hoopla and will gladly play along.

Located in Spirit Lake, the Dickinson County Museum was the first Iowa museum to be housed in a former railroad depot. If you're like me, you shake your head in wonderment and say, "So what?" then hightail it to the Higgins Museum in Okoboji proper where the largest banking museum in the Midwest is located. There you can watch actors posing as bank tellers make change. Now that's entertainment!

Finally, there is a fishing paraphernalia factory open for tours on some days. Go in and reassure yourself that it's worth it to spend $465 on tackle to catch a $1.65 fish.

Council Bluffs

Council Bluffs has been a railroad center since President Lincoln fixed the eastern terminus of the Union Pacific near the city in 1863. Boy, could that guy do wonders with a monkey wrench! In those days, good help was hard to find and if the president wanted something fixed right, he went out and did it himself.

Council Bluffs also has the Dodge House, a resplendent place where tour guides and custodians will chuck antiques and precious nicknacks that you feverishly attempt to dodge.

You will certainly remark "Golly!" when you visit the Pottawatamie County Jail and its famous "squirrel cage." A drum and metal cage allow the jailer to keep a continuous watch on all ten of the people incarcerated therein. It just keeps going round and round but never really gets anywhere, similar to a Dubuque City Council meeting.

Council Bluffs is across the Whogotthewaterrights River from Omaha. Midnight pranksters often erect billboards in Omaha: "If You Lived in Council Bluffs, You'd Be Literate by Now." There is much goodnatured joshing between the municipalities which only twice resulted in more than a few fatalities.

How was the town named? It is a tradition in Council Bluffs that each year the city council pretends to bring the GAMBLING DEMON into town by allowing a sport called dog racing. There is a well-known curse on Council Bluffs that goes, "Should dogs ever race, all Bluffers will lose face!" This means that citizens of Council Bluffs would gradually lose their facial features after giving in to the demon. Some say the Mormons provided this hex as they passed through toward civilized territory. Anyway, in years past, the Council Bluffs city council has had lots of laughs by bluffing a dog track ordinance.

Davenport

"Davenport, Gateway to Illinois" as the natives affectionately call it, is fond of its island arsenal in the middle of the Mississippi and the accompanying Browning Museum of Weaponry, a memorial to the Father of the Automatic Weapon. How would you like to go down in history with a title like that? Very impressive. And this is interesting: The Rock Island Arsenal is the only government installation left on earth *without* a stockpile of nuclear weapons. That's amazing. I know some people who get a tax break to store warheads in their basements; yet, the Davenport arsenal is still a holdout.

Davenport also has the Buffalo Bill Museum where, as you might expect, the original invoice for carpet cleaning after a herd of those scruffy creatures stampeded a local hotel is on display.

On a historical note, the first railroad from the East reached the Mississippi opposite Davenport in 1854. The first railroad bridge across the river was erected in 1954. According to one long-lived Davenporter, "Hey, we had some other things to do first!"

Lock and Dam No. 15 (what a clever way to name them!) is here too, which, all things considered, is better than Iowa City. You can tour this facility and learn from park rangers why flooding on the Great River occurs. Or you can save a few bucks and take my word for it — too much water.

By the way, the city is named for Jim Davenport, former shortstop of the San Francisco Giants.

In conclusion, I'd like to thank the Iowans I called randomly for this information. — Sunny Cal.

An Insider's Tour of Des Moines

Suppose you blow into Des Moines for a few days. What do you do? You probably visit the popular places but not much else. You visit the lush Botanical Center, impressive Living History Farms and my house. Maybe you see the State Capitol and have a snapshot taken next to a cannon or a legislator. Apart from that, it takes an insider's knowledge to get you to the right places in Des Moines. I'll be your guide.

Weather: Des Moines is affectionately known as "The City that Welcomes Bad Weather." This is obvious as you drive past many of our fine window repair businesses. Their signs are designed to taunt the Midwest Weather Fairy: BRING IN YOUR STORMS! In other words, we can handle anything thrown at us. But before venturing from your motel room, dress accordingly.

Native Dress: Des Moines is also known as "The City of Some Sartorial Distinction." To fit in, you should dress like the natives. For example, I usually wear a pinstripe suit, wing tips and no socks.

Entertainment: Of course, you could frequent the many four-star night spots of Des Moines and have a great time. But where is your sense of adventure? Have you ever attended a beheading? Here's how it goes:

"Where are you going, John?"

"I be heading to a maul, I reckon."

Mauls: So called because shoppers constantly grapple with each other for outstanding bargains. For instance, I recently got into a tussle over something we used to call an "unmentionable" but now it's practically all we talk about. You know, a frilly, intimate underthing — the less material involved, the more it costs. That kind. And the salesperson told me this was a genuine *Hawkeye* unmentionable for $199.99 already gift-wrapped. What a steal! And you know how *anything* Hawkeye sells in Iowa. So I won the tussle and took it home (the skimpy unmentionable, not the tussle). WOW! There was literally nothing to it. To the untrained eye it may have seemed that there was nothing in the gift box. But you have to understand the laws of skimpiness and Hawkeye mania to really appreciate what I got for a very foolish price. Very foolish.

An Insider's Tour of Des Moines

ADORING THRONGS AND WOLFHOUND THAT FOUNDED DES MOINES

Language: The term "Watch Your Language!" was coined in Des Moines because during winter (September through June) you can actually see your words freeze. Composition contests are often held, with participants filling the Capital City atmosphere with entire paragraphs before shards of shattered words crack and fall to earth. If someone would "like a word with you" or if you "have words" in Des Moines, it can be a beautiful experience.

Another language peculiarity can be found in the following sentence: "Yup, I reckon after the maul we could mosey on up to see the governor."

Renting a Mosey: These are tough times for Des Moines mosey drivers — you rarely see one on the streets. There is, however, a regular mosey run to the Tyrannical Center.

The Tyrannical Center: Des Moines is the home of the nation's first smell-easy. Before insurance and government came along, our biggest industry used to be flower arranging. The infamous Pondweed family used to arrange bouquets the way the underworld now arranges football games and Heisman Trophy winners. The Pondweeds were shrewd and surrounded themselves with fragrant Touch-Me-Nots during Pollination (1919-1933). The Tyrannical Center recreates the Pollination era from 1919 through the repeal of Pollination. If you can't remember the era yourself, ask your grandfather what it was like to sneak around in order to smell the roses.

Special Events: Plan to be here for KADDYWAUMPUS DAYS when we spell "Des Moines" sideways, swagger in our pinstripe suits, swill beer and sneer at sock salesmen. Or attend our famous 12K Run in which a dozen dignitaries dress up as a letter of the alphabet and dash past Adoring Throngs. And be sure to enter the GET LOST IN THE SKYWALKS COMPETITION. You can win valuable prizes if you're never found.

A Local Celebrity: His name is Adoring Throngs, master of disguise and ubiquitousness. He can be in several different places simultaneously and can be hundreds of different people. This has long covered up the truth about Des Moines' population: Most people don't know we've only got 13 people here. Needless to say, especially during visits by big-name politicians, Throngs does a swell job.

Night Life: Be sure to catch a floor show at any of our hot night spots. A full evening on the town can include linoleum, hardwood and carpet. For cement floors, obviously, there is no cover.

The State Fare: Legend has it that one day the Master of the Solar System got angry and said, "Hey, Iowa, do you think you can ride through the universe for free? Pay up." So every year since then we've taken our best animals, produce and displays to Des Moines and put on a festival to pay the freight for our state.

Arf and Silence Centers: On display at the Arf Center is a replica of the wolfhound that founded Des Moines. Also, Des Moinesians have known for years that silence is golden and that some people are willing to pay big bucks for a little peace and quiet. Still in its developmental stages, the Silence Center could very well produce that long-sought cash crop. (But keep it quiet).

Buy Iowa: Before you leave, don't forget to put in a bid on our state. By now, you've undoubtedly heard of the BUY IOWA campaign. It's for sale, I guess. And anyone would be proud to own it.

Driving in Des Moines

Fewer challenges are more demanding than driving in Des Moines. The following are a few tips and insights for vehicular and personal preservation while negotiating the city's thoroughfares:

Personalities: Des Moines drivers are among the most polite in the nation. While we have our share of backed-up and slow-moving traffic, we also have our share of "Good Eggs." Good Eggs make it a point to stop and wave on anyone frantically attempting to make a left turn across traffic. Unfortunately, there are two other personalities in Des Moines who like to crack the Good Eggs. The first is the IRATE, RED-FACED FIST SHAKER AND HORN-BLOWER (IRFFSH). This self-righteous member of the species inevitably ends up behind a Good Egg and always utters enough epithets to shame a sailor. The IRFFSH driver believes that God intended for some people to be forever stranded in the left-hand lane of life and to allow one across the traffic is a violation of the natural order of things. However, if, on another occasion, an IRFFSH is behind the turner and wishes to turn himself, he is immediately transformed into a BIWNRFCC, a BARRELING IDIOT WITH NO REGARD FOR COMMON COURTESY. If a Good Egg lets one through, the BIWNRFCC reasons, a Good Egg will allow dozens more to partake of his generosity. This sometimes results in what is known in Des Moines as a "collision." To further complicate matters, the IRFFSH is always in a Hurry and decides to zip past the Good Egg. This illegal passing maneuver often results in what is known as a "pile-up," with the IRFFSH the only one to escape—usually by way of the sidewalk.

A Hurry: Have you ever been in a Hurry? It is like a speeding bullet, only bigger and more dangerous. They ought to make a car by that name: "People will take notice and let you through—because (close-up of dashing IRFFSH couple uttering epithets, followed by close-up of several shame-faced sailors)...you're in a HURRY!

Anything Goes Zone: Outsiders beware. If you enter the *Anything Goes Zone*, there are no traffic rules. The *Zone* surrounds the State Capitol building, where unsuspecting motorists suddenly encounter a malady known as *Legislative Immunity*. This means our lawmakers can't get busted for tooling down the road at warp speed. But you can—if you're in their way.

The Freeway: The McVicar Freeway is the city's main artery; and it gets you where you want to go—fast. Unless a flake of snow falls or somebody is off on the shoulder fixing a tire. Then the CG's (Creeping Gawkers) take over. When this happens, plan to write your life story in the dust on the dash or finish your Ph.D. dissertation. It's going to be a while.

By the way, don't ask for the McVicar Freeway by name. Few Des Moinesians will know what you're talking about. Refer to it as "235" or "The Big Ditch." This thoroughfare was named in honor of Arnie McVicar, who 32 years ago began his search for a city parking place and, to the best of my knowledge, is still orbiting the city.

Parking: Everything that can be is metered. Sometimes it is best to park away from the downtown and take the bus. Some routes are what they call *Express*, which means they only take you a little out of the way before you arrive downtown—to Marshalltown, for example.

Vets Parking: Here is the rule-of-thumb (so-called because often you must hitchhike back to Vets): The farther away you park from Vets Auditorium, the more it costs. That makes sense. Latecomers to an event should have to pay for their tardiness. I know a guy who paid nearly $500 for a spot, but found out he was closer to Omaha and decided to attend an event there instead.

Maul Parking: They're supposed to, but how many maul employees really park far away from their jobs? Only those who fear for their jobs. The rest are so secure that when they get there early they park right on top of a fire hydrant in the tow-away zone where it says *You Will Be Prosecuted, Your Car Will Be Towed and Your Name Will Be Associated with The Iowa Legislature!* Powerful stuff. But it doesn't work. Face it: It's bad maul PR to bust anyone for a parking violation. The whole scene is a nasty one. You can get away with all kinds of creative parking at mauls. And what happens when some customers and employees get really audacious and start to park *inside* the maul? They fool us into thinking they're having a car show.

Ramps: Des Moines ramps look so good they are mistaken for buildings. And why not? You pay $15,000 for a stripped down American compact and you expect to get your dents and scratches in a classy place.

Underground Parking: We've all

Driving in Des Moines

WELCOME TO OUR RAMP

heard of someone so important that he has an underground, private and personally marked parking spot in a downtown building. Most Des Moinesians don't flaunt this; they are usually content to have identifying parking stickers the size of a bus windshield:

UNDERGROUND EXECUTIVE PARKING PRIVILEGES FOR A SIX-FIGURE INCOME PERSON. With such a sticker, it's hard to see out of the back of the car. But what do they care? That's the chauffeur's problem.

Orbit Shock: This occurs as you orbit a city block against all odds, hoping a metered spot will miraculously open up, saving you the $10 for-the-first-fifteen-minutes ramp fee. Normally, you have a better chance of winning $10 million in the Iowa Lottery than you do of finding a spot while in orbit. But...suddenly..there it is! The opening of a lifetime. You lick your chops and pull up to parallel park. You put it in reverse, look back and...watch somebody in a VW Bug scoot into the space behind you.

Rush Minute: Chicago has its finest hour; Des Moines does not. We do, however, have one minute of every day where each and every person who works downtown dashes to his car and hits the streets. Consequently, everyone rushes for a minute and sits for an hour.

The Finale: Crashing an Automatic Arm: Sooner or later you're bound to do it. It's a class struggle—the have's versus the have-nots. Sure you can fake it for awhile with your phony UNDERGROUND EXECUTIVE

PARKING PRIVILEGES (JUST VISITING THIS INADEQUATE SPACE) oversized sticker. But eventually you're going to get fed up after a scrubbed orbit, a terrifying whirl in the *Anything Goes Zone*, a dent in a ramp, a fist shaking session with an IRFFSH, a tow-away, a broken meter, and an encounter or two with Rush Minute. You're going to take on the hungry ABGPWYFUEPP's—THE ABOVE GROUND PARKERS WHO YEARN FOR UNDERGROUND EXECUTIVE PARKING PRIVILEGES. You're going to crash the ABGFWYFUEPPs' automatic arm—the one that looks like a cheap railroad crossing marker. And you're going to make the siren go off. And you're going to have thousands of frustrated ABGPWYFUEPP's descend upon your vehicle, shaking it wildly like demons possessed, pressing their flaring nostrils against your window. And you will never be heard from again.

Take the bus.

The Newspaper Iowa Descends Upon

Iowa Bore
by Shucks Oftenboring

I

I remember a bizarre experience with the *Resister*, "The Newspaper Iowa Descends Upon". ("They can't print that! Moida da bums!") I was working the day watch on the massage parlor ads when we got the call: The stubble fields had come to Iowa.

Stubble, Iowa's long-awaited third crop. Stubble, a chance for any man's face to look unkempt, unshorn, in style and, eventually, like Karl Marx's. Yes, it is downright communist and the *Resister*, with the appropriate consents from our new owner, Corporate, editorialized against the stubble phenomenon. We also printed pictures of uncooperative Iowa legislators next to nasty stubble stories: STUBBLE TROUBLE: DOES THIS LEGISLATOR ITCH TO RUIN IOWA? Of course, buried in the tenth paragraph is the answer: "Probably not." But who reads down to the tenth paragraph? We feel we are objective. And who's to say we aren't doing a good job? For my money, only Corporate.

Why fight a fad that will surely be dead by sundown, you ask. Because we're the *Resister*. Our motto: WE DO WHAT WE PLEASE (IF CORPORATE AGREES). When convenient, the First Amendment is our bastion of strength. In this case, we had a slew of advertisers who were downright opposed to a crop they couldn't capitalize on. O.K., you sell a pair of trimming shears, a few barrels of butch wax and a brush or two. You call that capital intensive?

I decided to cover the story. As is the case on all stories, a press agent, a photographer, three lawyers and throngs of well-wishers and worshippers accompanied me. About a dozen of our 113 editorial writers went along; most of them had never been out of the office.

I can't go anywhere anymore without being recognized. I'm Shucks Oftenboring, an Iowa media celebrity. Garter, our fishing columnist who writes "Worms, Worms, Worms," used to be popular too. But he's hardly a hot item since he went from the Opinion Page to across from the summaries of the soap opera plots, to who-knows-where next. Then there's Dade Yapsing, who writes the spicy "Capitol Chatter" and has most lawmakers shivering in their boots. You can never tell when something from the statehouse men's room will end up in his column — and it often does. Oh, and Prank Bowzer is starting to get a little attention. It started quite a while ago during the ouster of Marcos of the Phillistines. It seems that Bowzer had the good fortune of a two-hour airport stopover at the Phillistine International Airport. Naturally, when the Marcos thing broke, we were looking for a political analyst who had actually mingled with the Phillistine people. Bowzer said he might have bought a candy bar from someone who could have been a Phillistinian. That was enough for us.

I get my marching orders straight from Jakes Cannon, a big shot around here. Some people call him "Mr. Cannon," but I'm able to call him "Your Highness." Jakes doesn't care for stubble either, and his columns, when we can understand them, bristle with that fact. Not that Jakes can't write or isn't interesting or always belabors the same issues. No, not that! But we do have a little poem we pass around the office when he's taking a nap or talking to a legislator, which, of course, often amounts to the same thing:

> They say that the *Resister*,
> Is among the best in this great nation.
> But we all look forward to the heading on this column:
> "Jakes Cannon's on vacation!"

(O.K., we're journalists, not poets. The rhyme and meter are a little off, but so is the crew here at the *Resister*.)

II

"Grab a tart outta the glove compartment!" I yelled to my chauffeur. My annual Tart Tally brings in hundreds of tasty tarts to try. If I ever get out of journalism and into public service, I think I'd like to open a bakery.

We were a mile outside Des Moines, where for all practical purposes to the *Resister*, Iowa ends. Actually, the stubble field was in Muscatine County, but, hey, who wants to drive that far? For one thing, you'd get hungry and need a bigger glove compartment. Besides, we have a stringer down there who'll phone in some stuff we in the trade reluctantly refer to as "facts."

I was soon standing in the middle of a field with my entourage. I immediately tapped a credible and interesting source: I began to interview myself. The big question: How was I going to work the tart angle into a stubble story? After all, my stuff is true tart: light and puffy — maybe a little flaky. Well, maybe the editorial writers had an idea. I'd ask them as soon as they'd polished off that case of beer. Then it happened.

III

Over yonder. Wart Schlockwail, former columnist with our defunct sister publication, "Iowa's Best Dead Newspaper." We were onto the same story. I was angry. I suddenly wondered if we were using our resources wisely. (I don't know why I was thinking about oil and natural gas at a time like this!) All I know is that there's still fierce rivalry among reporters in the *Resister* club. But one common thread unifies us. One common concern for the future of free speech dominates our every waking minute: "Will I be the next to lose my job?" I quickly dashed off a memo on Schlockwail's whereabouts and instructed one of our lawyers to send it to Corporate. "And send a dozen roses and some fresh tarts!" I hastily added. Then something caught my eye.

I took a quick head count. Schlockwail had two more people in his entourage than I did. That's more than Princess Di or Johnny Rotten at the height of his punk career! I was incensed. (Yes, part of my followers' job is to dangle a burning urn at my feet and chant Latin, except when I'm taking my bongo lessons. It's hard to see your bongos with all that smoke.) Then it hit me.

IV

Of course! I didn't need tarts. I could work the bongo angle. Brilliant. Bongos and stubble go together. I'd do a Fifties reminiscence — something beatnik.

And I wouldn't be stepping on Schlockwail's toes. He always does the Forties. It was then I noticed.

V

Schlockwail was busy doing an interview. How insightful. *Talk* to somebody; involve the interviewee in the story. And what a superb choice, Dr. Ruthie Weisenheimer. I inched closer.

"I won't use the word 'whoopie' in my column when I mean 'orgasm,'" said Dr. Ruthie. By now Schlockwail and I were taking notes feverishly. Dr. Ruthie had come on board after the Corporate takeover. "And I won't use the word 'Shtubble' when I mean 'shtubble.' I'll use the word 'orgasm.' *That* sells newspapers!"

We were mesmerized. Someone who writes about something she appears never to have done. Hey, that sounds like our sports staff, who, at that very moment were rushing off a bus to join us. There was Smarts Handsome, Morley Puce, and Buck Turncoat, writer of the Prep Charade.

"What am I covering here?" shot Handsome as he handed his septer to a servant.

"Stubble" was our meek reply.

"Wait a minute!" thundered Turncoat. "What kind of playing field is this.

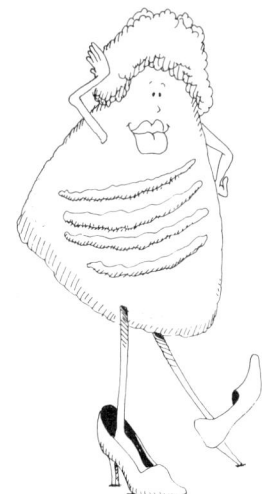

TYPICAL IOWA TART

I can't feel anything solid beneath my feet."

"It's the field of JOURNALISM!" everyone shouted in unison.

"So what does that have to do with sports?" said an obviously dismayed Puce.

"On a rising scale from zero to five stars, I'd have to give you boys a big, fat zero." It was June Bugge, critic-at-large. We were all surprised that Corporate hadn't relegated her to cleaning the computer terminals. Didn't they have somebody in New York who could read books and watch movies and remind us yokels we don't have any taste? Her rating formula was simple: Give at least four stars to any film with a foreign-sounding title. Is that so hard to do?

She immediately went for Ruthie's jugular.

"Dr. Weisenheimer, I was frankly appalled at the effusive ennui of the protagonist in a recent cinematic docudramatic portrayal of you as an Avon Lady who yearns to be a competitive weight lifter. The plot I found to be preposterous and the dialogue sophomoric. Only one word throughout: "Orgasm!" Why Katherine Hepburn ever consented..."

"Does that mean she didn't like it?" Ruthie whispered to me. So I did what I had to do: I lied. I said no. I said she loved it. I had to protect myself. Ruthie was our little bundle of big bucks — entertainment critical to the modern newspaper. Besides, I wasn't sure myself. Maybe it's time to get those tarts out of the glove compartment and put in a pocket dictionary.

VI

Suddenly a voice broke in.

"More color on the front page. More celebrity photos for People in the Nude!" Are you getting all this, Flacksbird?"

It was Jakes Cannon himself, with sidekick Jakes Flacksbird, who changed his first name shortly after Corporate came to town. (First names are like blue suits, they help you to look alike and sound alike, an important part of the Corporate Image.)

There was to be a meeting of the minds. I was asked to leave.

"I need more sex, Dr. Ruthie," pleaded Cannon. "Circulation is down." (He knows that his first job is to sell newspapers. If that doesn't happen, Jakes Cannon gets fired.)

"Maybe we take thousands of letters to the editor that we never print — or maybe the ones we reduce to half a sentence and we spice 'em up. We can do that under the First Amendment, can't we?" asked Cannon.

Everyone nodded, except for the lawyers, who nodded and shook their heads from side to side simultaneously. That takes uncanny coordination. I'm going to try that during bongo lessons.

"It'll cost," I heard someone shout.

"A free press doesn't come cheap," shot Cannon. And everyone bowed.

"And let's get Flyin' Ducky to do some cartoons to go along with the new Weisenheimerized letters to the editor," said Cannon.

"Ducky this and Ducky that!" mimicked a voice I knew I had heard before. "The way you talk, Cannon, everything's Ducky!"

Cannon got that "off with the heretic's head" look on his face until he realized it was someone who had already been subjected to that management style. It was the last "Overtly Cocky" columnist, Hoosier. He approached Cannon glowing, head intact.

(By this time, most of the *Resister* staff had assembled in the field, including late-arriving travel writer Baccardi and shutterbug Farewell, who get to brag about all their vacations and get paid for it too.)

Hoosier spoke. "Since banished, I have been living with genuine seekers of truth," he said. "I harbor no ill will. The extra-terrestrials treat me very well..."

As he spoke, a meteor-like shining orb came over the horizon and little green men emerged wearing little green eyeshades and uttering memorized lines from "The Imperative of Freedom: A Philosophy of Journalistic Autonomy" by John C. Merrill. I was dumbfounded. I wondered aloud what journalistic autonomy had to do with the *Resister*. Cannon glared at me.

Hoosier continued. "These beings have found the secret to journalistic freedom, the key to journalistic social responsibility and the recipe for a tasty low-calorie blueberry tart," Hoosier announced.

"You're *still* not funny," shot Cannon.

We were awestruck. My colleagues began firing questions at each other: "How can a pastry be low calorie?" "Do they use a butter substitute?"

We might have gotten a picture but our photographers don't like to carry around their cameras. They say it impairs spontaneous creativity. I guess I can understand that, although a half-page colorful tart shot would have looked great in our "Foods" section.

The awe continued until someone checked his watch.

"Off duty!" was the cry.

So we all went home. And Cannon told us that nothing should appear in the paper: "It ain't news unless the *Resister* says it is!"

A Cartographer's Dream

"Cartography?" My nephew had heard the word somewhere and wanted an explanation. As always, I was glad to share my vast knowledge: "Probably one of those grocery shopping vehicles from Eagles in Dubuque was left in a Hy-Vee lot in Des Moines. Some pranksters will stop at nothing."

My nephew now knows that cartography is the study of the migration patterns of grocery carts that get pushed astray. I've heard tell of a Super Valu cart being found in Argentina, which, when you think about it, is a long walk, especially if you bought ice cream: By the time you get near the equator, you're probably in trouble. But I guess supermarket bargains are worth the extra effort, even if you need a map.

Cartography is also, as I recently discovered, the art of making maps. I discovered this on the same day I sat in my office trying to concoct more goofy stuff and got a double brainstorm that crack journalists are famous for: First, "Why don't I *leave* my Des Moines office and go talk to somebody?" Second: "What if I try writing about a topic while using some semblance of research and insight?" Hey, I had never done either of those. It was going to be a big day.

All Respected Journalists Do This

If I go out, I go in style. So the first thing I did was secure the biggest, most expensive vehicle I could find. While sitting at the back of the bus, I peered out the window, scouring the landscape for the perfect person, place or thing to interview. I thought, "All respected journalists probably do this." Then I felt a pang of guilt: "That means we're missing some good stories if they're not on the regular bus routes!"

Was I a lazy journalist? The next thing I knew the bus driver was rousing me and saying I'd have to pay another 60 cents to go around again.

"You only go 'round once," I kept reminding myself. Another time would have put my expense allotment for this story over budget. So I hoofed it down to Locust Street where, unbeknownst to me, the cartography story awaited.

The sign above the storefront said MAPS. And the first thing I thought was, "Can a person make a go of it just by selling maps?" Actually, that's the second thing I thought. The first thing was, "Aren't maps those pieces of paper with colored lines all over them that you can turn over and use for a projection screen in a pinch?"

So I went in and met the owner of Roberts' Maps. The first thing I said when he said, "Hi, I'm the owner, Dwaine," was "No you're not!" But he seemed so sure of himself. "You're Robert!" I pressed. People who don't know their own names are the kind of people who push shopping carts to Argentina. But he persisted.

Can You Smile and Talk at the Same Time?

"My last name is Roberts," he smiled. I've often wondered why people do that. Can you really smile and talk at the same time? Try it. It looks like you're struggling to be polite but really want to bite someone's head off.

I was getting nowhere. Good thing I was in a map place. And Dwaine sure did know a lot about maps. To demonstrate that he was dealing with an educated man, I asked him an insightful question: "Can you use that inflatable, see-through globe over there as a beach ball?" That is also when I discovered that you can't make a go of it just by selling maps. You have to sell globes, too, especially ones through which you can stealthily view bikinis and, if you wish, the people in them.

Albania Drops In

At that point I was more than satisfied with the comprehensiveness of the interview, but Dwaine insisted on showing me around. Dwaine Roberts sure is enthusiastic about the map and globe business. He said the Secretary of Albania even dropped in and bought $200 worth. I forgot to ask if she had a shopping cart. My guess is that she went out to pick up the boss's laundry and wandered away from Albania, marveling at the storefronts or the hillside scenery and she finally realized she needed a map. This happens to me a lot. At any rate, the Secretary picked up some notes for diplomats, which Dwaine also sells. I wonder how many other Des Moines businesses can say they're equipped with background notes should an Albanian diplomat pop in? Pretty impressive.

The map store is a cartographer's dream. There are city maps. County maps, state maps, national maps, moon maps, treasure maps, and 7½ minute maps, so named because that's how long it takes to wrench one out of your glove compartment when you're whizzing all by yourself down a busy freeway.

Iowa Is Completely Mapped

The biggest scoop that Dwaine imparted was that Iowa has just been completely and officially mapped by the U.S. Geological Survey. So what was the rush? We've only been a state for 140 years. These Geological guys are no slouches; they're meticulous. Dwaine showed me a sample 7½ minute map and pointed out gulches, ravines, houses, ponds, potholes and abandoned shopping carts in the Scotch Ridge Quadrangle of Warren County. That's what I call being completely mapped. It was worth the wait. Never mind that they might have gotten us mixed up with South Dakota. They've got a lot of states to cover. Besides, the businesses of Warren County will certainly benefit from the increased tourist trade when everyone's combing the county looking for Mount Rushmore. But I'm not going out to look. Not until they get Babe Bisignano's face up there.

Anyway it was time for two final cartographic questions: "Why can't women read maps?" and "Do you sponsor folding classes?" These are important questions since the two biggest fights in my life centered on a missed exit and a clumped wad of colored paper that had once been a neatly folded map. Dwaine's visitors' register is signed by a woman: "Maps are fabulous

A SHOPPING CART

fun!" she wrote. Of course they are. Woman, if you want to see a man screw himself into the sidewalk out of sheer frustration, just pull out a map and ask for directions. Then crumple the whole thing up while pretending to fold it. There. You've fully destroyed his sacred sense of cartography. Enough said.

I was surprised to learn that hunters and fishermen frequent Roberts' Maps. I spied nary a hint of wild game! O.K., I'm not the most observant of crack journalists. But I know a good map when I see one.

Feelies

My favorites are the "feelies." That's what we used to call them in grade school. Actually, they're "raised relief"—the same kind of thing you feel when your teenager has finally left home. Dwaine also has what they call Peters Projection Maps that, according to a sign in the store, are "superior in their portrayal of proportions and size." Peters redid the world map because all past cartographers lied to us. In reality, the U.S. is no bigger than a pinhead on the map, the Soviet Union comprises 99 percent of the world's land mass and Africa has a long, droopy snout. The Peters Projection Map somehow doesn't look "right," but, sometimes, neither does reality.

My favorite specialty item for sale is the "Build Your Own Mount St. Helens." When I saw it, I erupted with joy. You can also "Rebuild the Hawaiian islands." And if you do, could you please make the hotel rates a little more reasonable?

Roberts' Maps is replete with map umbrellas, map backpacks and map duffel bags. They say "you can't take it with you," but I'm not so sure. Maybe Dwaine has a map...

No Longer A Forbidden World...

Did you have a favorite hangout when you were a kid? A malt shop? A garage? A pool hall? A lingerie boutique perhaps?

I swear, I recently walked past one of those places reputed to model lingerie for purchasers and I saw several teenage guys hanging around outside! And yes, I do know the difference between lingerie shop and a garage. At a lingerie shop, it is unlikely you will be greeted by a sweaty guy in greasy overalls with "Al" stitched to the pocket. Besides, I had just boned up on how to spot a lingerie shop. An Iowa newspaper I depend upon recently ran "How men can buy gifts of frilly, lacy lingerie."

Hard News

They refer to such stories as "hard news" because they run them on days when it's hard to come up with anything else. We're fortunate they devote space to public service features like "How men can buy gifts of frilly, lacy lingerie." Because of such fare, we are lucky enough to be raising a generation of young men who no longer frequent pool halls, malt shops, and garages. After all, a garage mechanic can teach you how to tighten a lug nut, but can he teach you how to behave in a lingerie boutique?

Catcalls of Encouragement

The kids I observed looked pretty sure of themselves and not at all embarrassed about their chosen hangout. They even offered catcalls of encouragement to an approaching male whose uncertain steps evinced embarrassment. "Come on in!" beckoned the boys' smiles. "Hey, this is no longer a forbidden world!" They must feel as we did when we chalked up our first pool cue or when the mechanic stopped shooing us away and let us fix a flat.

The newspaper story begins: *"The man walks into the forbidden, frilly world of lacy, skimpy lingerie, then blushes, takes a deep breath and tries not to act embarrassed. But, of course, he is. And, of course, he needs help."*

Lingerie. I never trust anything I can't pronounce phonetically. Yet, the phonetic pronunciation of "lingerie" does not exude the scandalously soft sizzle of satin tap pants and stretchy lace camisoles. But let the French pronunciation rumble seductively through your resonant vocal cords and exit through your lips in a rush of breathless sensuality and ...Whew! Then try to pronounce the words "burger and fries," "ratchet wrench" and "bumper pool" and it will become obvious why the last word with our kids is lingerie.

Is a Flannel Charmeuse Really So Ridiculous?

Amazing. Des Moines proper—and improper for that matter—consumes more lingerie than Anchorage, Juneau, Fairbanks and the upper reaches of the Yukon combined. O.K., you counter, that's really Flannel Country. But is the idea of a flannel charmeuse really so ridiculous?

Yes. Especially patterned flannel with Disney characters.

When I think of the word "consume," I think of those funtime licorice panties that are so appealing to the sweet tooth. See, people like Sgt. Preston don't consume a lot of sweets and a survivalist like Nanook of the North doesn't fret much about an instantaneous transformation into a fantasy sex goddess afforded by a slinky licorice teddy. That's why Des Moines is ahead in the consumption department, although I have no figures on discombobulation.

The newspaper article said that men who shop for lingerie are generally "discombobulated." This is utterly ridiculous. The Des Moines Police Vice Squad and the more than 500 males who comprise the Volunteer City-wide Lingerie Boutique Inspection Department assured me that discombobulation does not take place on these premises.

Pappalardo Types

The article goes on to quote a guy named Pappalardo, who, from the sound of his name, could probably stand to lose a few pounds himself before he expects his significant other to squeeze into some salty chemise. Pappalardo types are the ones who expect visions of wonderment and allure when they themselves are not properly attired. If you shell out 200 smackers for a silk bias-cut Jean Harlow nightgown and you dress like Freddy the Freeloader fresh from a back-alley poker game, you deserve what you get.

And get this: A direct, unaltered quote from the article: "When buying lingerie, men 'usually will go for something better, finer, prettier than the woman herself.'" What an insult! Yes, this means more than one Iowa man has run off with the likes of a poly-satin kimono-top pajama set or something salaciously similar. I blame the governor.

"It can't happen here!" you say. But that's what they said about denim. Here are a few questions and answers:

How do you buy lingerie for a woman who could stand to lose a few pounds? You've heard of people like this—so hefty, when they stand they lose a few pounds. The big question is *where* do you buy a suitable garment? At the Naughty-but-Nice Petticoat and Awning Company in Ames.

How can you be sure you've selected the right size? You have heard the old adage that people resemble their pets. Well, try that lacy bodice-hugger on the dog; chances are, one size fits all anyway.

And how do you handle kids who really should be hanging out in pool halls? Give them enough money to go away and buy a pool hall. Or if you are really loaded, give them enough money to pay a mechanic for an hour.

Can you read up on this kind of thing? Yes, the newspaper cites the book, "Enticements: How to look fabulous in lingerie." Actually, we're becoming so casual about these matters, you're likely to find an article even in *Popular Mechanics*, especially if circulation is down.

For what occasions should lingerie be purchased? Valentine's Day is nice. Christmas is thoughtful. Or after your arrest for allowing the dog to prance up

NINE OF THE TEN IOWA MEN WHO PERSONALLY SELECTED LINGERIE LAST YEAR LOOKED LIKE THIS.

Grand Avenue in a lacy bodice hugger.

What about a fit? Will your significant other throw one when she discovers you spent the Mercedes money on a moo-moo that shines in the dark? Not if it fits properly. By the way, short women look taller in full-length robes and heels. Tall women look taller in full-length robes and heels, too.

Who sells the stuff? These days, everybody. Even the QuickStop has a small but enticing line, as do some plumbing concerns and a few bait shops.

Finally, now that we've unabashedly entered the forbidden world of skimpy lingerie, how do you make a purchase? It is best to order by mail. Be sure to use a phony name and an address somewhere in the upper reaches of the Yukon. And don't ever be caught dead in a lingerie boutique.

Real Men Mow and Fry Out

An unscientific survey recently asked Iowa men the question, "During a fire in your home, which items would you try to save?" Of course, there were the predictable answers: photo albums, stock certificates and pin-ups of Dolly Parton. But several respondents named the lawn mower and the barbecue grill. This made me attentive and curious. And that doesn't happen very often.

I can understand why a microwave/TV combination would be named. What good is it to watch the Saturday afternoon ball game without stuffing your face? But the mower and grill? What's the connection?

The Mower

What is it that truly brings out the man in an Iowa man — besides a carnival barker's taunting invitation to wrestle a starving Kodiak bear? That's right, the lawn mower. I'm sorry, females, but you just don't have the same kind of relationship with the sheering machine. When you mow, you see the act as utilitarian and maybe a tan. When we mow, we tame and preen.

What is a lawn? People have received Ph.D.s for answering such questions, but I'll keep it simple. A lawn is a symbol of tamed wilderness. Therefore, mowing serves to satisfy man's primeval urge to blaze trails and conquer menacing underbrush. Show me a man with an unkempt lawn and I'll show you a discombobulated Daniel Boone. Chances are, his whole world is out of whack.

The mower, then, is the machete in the jungle, the Neanderthal's club, the knight's lance, the park ranger's Weed Eater. The man behind the machine is the conquerer and caretaker of verdant turf. Read the instructions sometime that come with a new Lawn Person: "Congratulations: You have purchased an outstanding machine that will give you thousands of trouble-free hours of conquering and taking care of verdant turf..." Which brings me to the preening part.

Preening, Primping and Piddling

Listen to yourself sometime. "Darling, I'm going out to cut the lawn." Did you say "cut"? No, you really said "preen." Your wife heard "preen." Your inflection really said "preen," not "cut." It's just that "preen" doesn't happen to be one of the three hundred words that comprise the American macho vocabulary. You say cut; but you mean preen.

A real man will spend from fifty to sixty hours per week on his lawn. He will sneak out in the middle of the night just to get in some extra time preening, primping or just piddling. In Iowa, he has less than six months of prime taming and preening time. The other six months he spends in the basement tuning and shining the mower, fondly recollecting past mowing experiences and contemplating the vast world of fertilizers. It comes as no surprise, then, to learn that the third thing the man would save would be his Scott's spreader. (Side note: We men spend millions of dollars annually on fertilizer and crab grass control agents. Know what? They're all placebos. Made up of 100 percent inert ingredients, similar to the brains of the guys who answered "the mower and barbecue grill" in the aforementioned survey. Did you *really* think a tiny pellet could discriminate between a genuine blade of grass and a blade of crab grass? Get serious.) (Second side note: This is not to say that lawn chemicals are not essential to the male psyche. Next time, watch a guy as he paternalistically pushes a spreader stocked with placebos. It looks just like he's pushing a baby carriage!)

But what becomes of a man without a lawn? He must fry out.

The Grill

Did you ever notice all the options you can get on lawn mowers and barbecue grills? Some men pay more for their mowers and their grills than they do for their wardrobes. And it shows. For example, look at all the paraphernalia on your average grill: A stick shift to raise and lower the griddle, wheels to maneuver your grill into tight places, and a rear view mirror to get a jump on a neighbor coming to complain about all the smoke. Real men need well-equipped grills, especially real men without a mower.

Frying out. I first heard that phrase in Sheboygan, Wisconsin and I was confused. I had heard of people "steaming inside" and others who got "boiling mad." Someone who was "frying out," I reckoned, really must be showing signs of perturbation. In reality, however, frying out is synonymous with what Iowans call "cooking out" or "charring beyond recognition a very expensive piece of meat."

A man does not become a *real* man until he has fried out, or at least cooked someone else's goose. Harken back to the days of the cave man who prized his lawn and cherished his ability to roast a mastadon to perfection. We men have a gene or two that compels us to sear our foods into submission and we have a fierce pride that says everyone at the table must acknowledge our prowess at frying out. But before the example, first the smoke.

Typical Fry Out Exchange

You are not effective at frying out unless your entire block is engulfed in smoke. The acid test: Can you see your neighbor's home at all? Has he called the fire department? Is it a three-alarm fry out? *Typical real man fry out exchange at the office Monday morning:*

"I had two ladder trucks at my place yesterday..."

"You think that's something? I had motorists fogged out all the way to Ames..."

Here's the fierce pride example: A real man invites a friend to dinner. Let us suppose the friend did not see the barbecue grill or the pumper trucks or the pile-up on I-35. The friend sits down at the table and asks, "What are we having?" The real man says nothing. If the friend says, "Wow, this sure has a fried-out taste!" he is a friend for life. If he says, "Did you do this in the microwave?" the real man feels ashamed and perhaps skewers him.

Have you noticed that the only time you'll ever see a man wearing an apron is when he's frying out? And have you ever answered the question, "How would you like yours done?" knowing full well that there is only one way — burnt beyond belief? And have you ever tried to find fresh mastadon in the supermarket?

Look, nobody said being a real man is easy. But you know you've got it made when Sunday rolls around and the mower hums, the ball game blares, your quarry sizzles on the grill and your wife has a back-up meal in the microwave.

The Heavyweight State

Researchers have determined that some of us are predisposed to huskiness. Nothing wrong with that; it's in the genes. Some doctors say a bit of blubber is good to have around—so to speak—in case of illness or a malted milk embargo. So why is it that we're so obsessed with slender?

Iowa is on the verge of something big. We need to position ourselves in the minds of Americans as "The Heavyweight State." We need to attract and retain those Last-Ditch-Diet dropouts. We've got plenty to gain and nothing to lose.

First, we need a bona-fide, corn-fed researcher to pronounce that the Iowa environment is ultra-healthful for those of us who bloat a bit. In fact, I am not ashamed to admit that I retain water. Right now I'm retaining Lake Okoboji. (Take a look. It's gone!)

Big Bones are Beautiful!

Our research authority will make us feel good about ourselves and help us further our quest to also be called "The Euphemism State." For example, when you go to California you are automatically shamed into losing ten pounds and you feel faint. When you come to Iowa, we call you "big-boned" and leave you alone. And that's marketable. We could even go so far as to greet tourists and potential settlers at the borders with a side of beef and something from Sara Lee. Anyway, here are a few big ideas for "The Heavyweight State:"

Weight Gaining: "Homeclowning '88" will be the rage. So let's piggyback a "Weight Gaining '88" promotion. Face the facts: The only jokers who will actually come home to Iowa, after years of writing mimeographed Christmas letters filled with lies about the sweet life, are those with tangible proof of the sweet life. So do you think that anyone who isn't fashionably svelte is going to drag his carcass back to Iowa? Not unless we offer some encouragement. Suppose we say that nobody is allowed across the Mississippi without proof that they've put on ten pounds since they left. Or suppose we don't let them out of Omaha without taking a pinch test. They'll all do it. Who wants to be stranded in Omaha? Maybe we demand to see an old driver's license or a World War II uniform photo for proof. Maybe.

Fat City: We should rename Des Moines. If this truly is "The Surprising Place," let's really surprise homecomers:

At a Minnesota gas station: "I haven't been back to Iowa for decades, but I seem to remember a place called Des Moines. I just can't locate it on this map."

(Attendant pores over map.) "Nope, I don't see no Deez Moinz either. You might wanna try and ask up there (It's actually "down there," but remember, this guy is from Minnesota...) ta Fat City; they might know."

Fat Chance: Doesn't that have a better ring to it than the "Iowa Lottery?"

Rewrite the Chubby Charts: Some states rewrite history. We don't need to aim that high. But let's do everyone a favor and rewrite the chubby charts. Let's make a chart that accounts for heredity, metabolism, the Iowa environment and, most importantly, vanity. As the great Horace Hefty advised, "Gain weight, young man!" Then weigh yourself and take...

The New Iowa Realistic Weight Assessment Scale

1. **Height:** Subtract 5 pounds if you have some.
2. **Frame:** Are your bones big? (Test: Do they fit under your skin? Well, then they must be big because skin stretches a lot. Subtract 10 pounds.)
3. **Genetic Background:** Subtract 5 pounds if you have inherited good looks. (Let's face something else—everybody will take 5 on this one.) Subtract 10 pounds if you have inherited great stares. And don't even bother to weigh yourself if you have inherited catcalls from construction workers.
4. **Transportation:** Do you "carry yourself" well? That's a real trick. You have to be a contortionist. And they're always skinny. Subtract 50 pounds and consider joining the circus.
5. **Constitution and Frame:** Subtract 5 pounds if you know who framed the Constitution.
6. **Gravity Differential:** The pull of gravity is different in Iowa. Subtract 20 pounds.
7. **Iowa Winters:** You'll need at least 25 pounds of insulation to make it through one. So those pounds don't count. Subtract them.
8. **Sex:** Subtract 10 pounds if you participate. Subtract 15 pounds if you desire to: after all, frenzied fantasy is hard work!
9. **Consumption Habits:** Sorry, but add five pounds if you currently have in your possession more than a dozen unexpired Pizza Hut coupons. (#9 is not to be used with any other category; void where prohibited.)
10. **Metabolism:** You know how they say that some people are skinny because they burn calories faster than

The Heavyweight State

other poor slobs? They usually say it with a gloating sneer, because the "they" are usually the metabolic mutants I'm talking about. "I can eat anything (gloat!) and I never gain a pound! (sneer)" Subtract 10 pounds if you hate these people as much as I do.

There. You have now arrived at your ideal Iowa weight. But what happens if you've subtracted more pounds than you actually weigh? Great! This means you don't exist, which means they're going to have a hell of a time proving that you have to pay taxes. And that's yet another drawing card for our state!

The "Shoes" Comprehensive Exam

So *you think you read the book carefully. And you think you know a lot about Iowa? Let's find out. Take the following quiz:*

1. Name the state capital:
  A. Jason
  B. Nathan
  C. Josh
  D. Stephanie

2. Name the state shoe:
  A. Don't be silly; there is a state sock but no state shoe.

3. O.K., then name the state shoe song:
  A. What's Shoe Doing in My World?
  B. Shoe City Shoe
  C. Folsom Prison Shoes
  D. Baby It's Shoe

4. What has been the state legislature's greatest accomplishment in recent years?
  A. Changing the state motto to "Oh, What the Hell!"
  B. Enlarging the boys' basketball to the size of a beached whale
  C. Telling the State Bureau of Tourism to get off their butts and begin a "Steal A Better Class of Towel in Iowa" campaign
  D. Regular adjournment

5. Identify the governor of Iowa:
  A. He can no longer be identified because these days he has taken to wearing pantyhose over his head during public appearances.

6. What is the state cheer?
  A. Horseshoe, gumshoe, clodhopper, cleat: Shoes to live in Iowa—it sure is neat!
  B. Two bits, four bits, six bits, a dollar. All for price supports, stand up and bitch about it!
  C. We used to be in the black; now we're in the red. Do you think that's why—the guv wears pantyhose on his head?

7. You have lived in this state all your life. Your spouse comes home and announces that Sioux City has seceded from Iowa. You:
  A. Wonder who finally filled out all the forms.

The "Shoes" Comprehensive Exam

B. Go look up the word "seceded."
C. Go look up the words "Sioux City."
D. Invoke the new state motto (See question #4, option "A")

8. What is the state song?
A. "Don't Bother Me, I'm from Iowa"
B. "It's No Bother, I'm from Iowa"
C. "It Bothers Me that I'm from Iowa"
D. "Why Do We Even Bother with a State Song?"

9. "Ask Dr. Ruth" runs in our state-wide newspaper. This column is:
A. porno masquerading as self-help
B. self-help masquerading as porno
C. a clever way to raise circulation
D. a clever way to raise blood pressure, too

10. What was the message in the Iowa Bore column?
A. There's more than one way to bake a tart.
B. Little green men do wear little green eyeshades.
C. Journalists are lousy poets.
D. Avon ladies can be weight lifters.
E. Hoosier is still not funny.

11. In Iowa, is it against the law to laugh at your own jokes?
A. Yes, and the penalty is that you must wear a seed corn cap.
B. Yes. That's why you got married, wasn't it?

12. What is a lawn?
A. a symbol of tamed wilderness
B. a preening, primping and piddling place packed with placebos
C. only Ph.D.s can adequately answer this question

13. You walk into an Iowa lingerie boutique. You ask...
A. what they have in a pink chemise
B. who they have in a pink chemise
C. what they feed a pink chemise
D. if it's legal in Iowa to marry a poly-satin kimono-top pajama set
E. what they've got in flannel with Disney characters

14. You find the pink chemise. You say...
A. "Hey, this is ten bucks cheaper at the bait shop!"
B. "Would Al look silly with one of these over his coveralls!"
C. "Do you have anything that hides thunder thighs?"
D. "Are you sure Sgt. Preston bought one of these for Nanook of the North?"
E. "Where'd the dog go? I want him to try this on."
F. "Wrap it up and send it to this address in the Yukon."

The "Shoes" Comprehensive Exam

15. How should you react if your clothes start speaking about the many virtues of Iowa?

A. Run and get a tape recorder; talking clothes are rare.

B. Keep them talking and call 911 for a tailor.

C. Tell your shorts to "Shut Up!"

16. When will Iowa get its first naked car wash?

A. When your clothes start to talk.

B. I don't know, but you can bet it won't be located in Mingo.

C. I don't know, but when it does happen, you can bet that washing the car will beat out mowing the lawn and frying out as an Iowa guy's favorite pastime.

17. What is the funniest joke in Iowa?

A. your job
B. your salary
C. your house payments
D. all of the above
E. all of the above plus your marriage

18. Which of the following is not an essential to bring night fishing?

A. bait
B. a fishing pole
C. your Blue Cross card
D. a console color TV
E. a dictionary of dirty words

19. Which is the best example of awfulizing in your C-Zone?

A. The universe will explode before I have a chance to organize my sock drawer.

B. I will never do a decent doodle and nobody will ever compliment my fried-out food.

C. I will be eaten alive by a giant dust bunny in my closet.

20. What did you learn from the NEW IOWA REALISTIC WEIGHT ASSESSMENT SCALE?

A. that you don't retain half as much water as the author

B. that you don't exist

C. that even if you didn't exist, you're still convinced you'd retain water

D. that the circus is a viable career option

21. What did you learn from this book?

A. that pine needles breed in car trunks

B. that one of Radar O'Reilly's hampsters is smart enough to run a bowling alley

C. that you can purchase a farmer at a farmers' market

D. that $4.95 was way too much to pay for this book

The "Shoes" Comprehensive Exam

22. What did you not learn from this book?

A. that direct descendants of Ivan the Terrible run a Taco John's in Davenport

B. that former Iowan Andy Williams' portrait is not on the $100,000 bill, but if Woodrow Wilson is ever proven to have had a girlfriend named "Kitten," Williams has a shot at it

C. Fidel Castro used to be a big fan of Household Hints from Heloise on WHO Radio until she started spouting subliminal anti-communist slurs during baking soda tips

D. that the mint-green leisure suit was invented in Grundy Center

Score Interpretation

Score no points for each "A" answer, 2 points for each "B" answer, and 4 points for all other answers.
If you got:

—Between 0 and 10 points: You are hardly aware of Iowa and totally unaware of yourself. Nobody else is aware of you either. Check to see if you're invisible.

—11 to 29 points: You know something about Iowa, but not enough to brag about and you're probably from Mason City.

—29 to 49 points: You are a sensitive and discerning individual and a better person for having read this book, which you will now recommend to your friends.

—50 and over: There is no doubt about it: You cheated on this quiz. Go spend the rest of your life in Minnesota.

RADAR'S HAMPSTER BOWLS A FEW FRAMES IN HIS FAVORITE LEISURE SUIT

Index

A
Avon Lady, 50

B
booby for a boss, 0

C
calls, cat, 56
Carson, Johnny, 29
Castro, Fidel, 68
charts, chubby, 63
Collins, Joan, 16

D
daughter, farmer's, 11
Diet, Last-Ditch, 62

E
Eggs, Good, 42
"Eroticism in Early American Verse," 25

F
feelies, 54

G
Gambling, Demon, 37
globes to view bikinis, 53
gone, Lake Okoboji, 62

H
hobo life career option, 19

J
Johnson, Don, 24

L
living, clean, 4
loafers, 14
lottery, 10
lusts and riches, 7

M
marijuana, 35
Marx, Karl, 46
MEGASEX, 2
Mingo, 67

N
Naughty-but-Nice Petticoat and Awning Company, 58
Nicholson, Jack, 15

O
Olson, Mrs., 13
orbit shock, 44

P
Phillistines, The, 47

R
Radar's Teddy Bear, 33

S
Shebang, National Sheep, 20
shorts, talking, 67
sleet buzzard, slickback, 23

T
Tart Tally, annual, 47
temptress, 5
torture, 15

U
Up!, Surf's, 22

W
warsh, 9
water, too much, 38